I0798684

REMEMBERING

# Jefferson County

# REMEMBERING Jefferson County

## *From Pioneers to Aviators*

RANDON W. BARTLEY

THE History PRESS

Published by The History Press
Charleston, SC 29403
www.historypress.net



First published 2009

Manufactured in the United States

ISBN 978.1.59629.686.2

Library of Congress Cataloging-in-Publication Data

Bartley, Randon W.
Remembering Jefferson County : from pioneers to aviators / Randon W. Bartley.
p. cm.
Includes bibliographical references and index.
ISBN 978-1-59629-686-2 (alk. paper)
1. Jefferson County (Pa.)--History. 2. Jefferson County (Pa.)--Biography. I. Title.
F157.J4B37 2009
974.8'62--dc22
2009015774

This work is dedicated to the two women in my life:
my mother, June Bartley Miller, who encouraged me to read,
and my wife, Barb, who has indulged my passion for words.

# Contents

# Preface

This work is not intended to be a definitive history of Jefferson County. It is intended to entertain and, hopefully, inform the reader of a few selected incidents in our shared past. Quite often the history of rural areas of this nation is overlooked and discounted in the fervor to tell the larger story. But history is about people, individuals who are compelled to do something out of the ordinary. For that they should be recognized. It is my hope that this work has recognized a few of those people.

This work was completed with the aid of several friends, and to them I would extend my sincere gratitude. My thanks to David Taylor, Ken Burkett, Dennis Bonavita and Theresa Costa at the the Jefferson County Historical Society, who have been invaluable in the pursuit of illusive images.

I have used the files of the various Brookville newspapers as a primary source for many of these chapters. I am indebted to those men and women who wrote those pages, recording history as it happened.

# Part I

# Tales from the Pioneers

## A Man in the Wilderness Called Moses

Among the tombstones in the old Jefferson Cemetery is that of one of the pioneer settlers of Jefferson County—Moses Knapp. He was a pioneer in the wilderness and business of Jefferson County.

In her *History of Jefferson County*, Kate Scott tells us that Moses Knapp came to Jefferson County in 1797 with Samuel Scott and Andrew and Joseph Barnett. Knapp was about nineteen years old and was the adopted son of Scott, from whom he learned the millwright trade.

A year or two later, he left his friends at Port Barnett and built a mill for himself on the North Fork, near the site of the old Litch mill, making Moses Knapp the first settler in Brookville.

In the fall of that year, he went to Indiana to attend one term of school. There he met Susan Matson, a daughter of Uriah Matson (who later moved to Brookville).

Knapp married Susan and brought his new bride back to his cabin on the North Fork. In 1801, the first of the couple's eleven children, Polly, was born. After a few years, he sold the mill and his "betterments" and built another cabin at the mouth of the North Fork. He also built a new mill on what was then known as Knapp's Run (now Five Mile Run).

He built a log gristmill with a run of stones. The new mill was a marvel of pioneer technology. Scott says that the water was gathered by a wing dam of brush and stones. The water was brought into a chute that passed it under a large "undershot" water wheel with a "face-geer" wheel upon the water wheel shaft, "mashed" into a "trundle-head" on the spindle that carried the revolving stones and comprised the "primitive propelling machinery."

The mill was often taxed to the utmost according to Scott, and the pioneers brought their harvest from twenty or thirty miles around. Knapp lived there from 1807 until 1818, when he moved to Clover Township. Knapp built a total of seven mills: two on the North Fork, one on Knapp's Run and four on Red Bank Creek.

About 1819, Knapp built a sawmill in what is now Baxter. This mill was sold eight times before Richard Baxter bought the foundation of the mill in 1854.

The move to Clover also brought another distinction to Moses Knapp. He was the first person in the county to undergo a "capital surgical operation." While building the Baxter mill, a tree fell on Knapp, crushing his foot and leg. Drs. Newton and Rankin were called and quickly determined that an amputation was in order. They sent to Indiana and Kittaning for the necessary instruments but, unable to locate the tools, proceeded with a hunting knife and carpenter's saw. The flesh was cut "square off," leaving Knapp with a "tender stump."

In 1821, Knapp bought a quantity of land from the Holland Land Company in Clover Township. A portion of that property later became the village of Dowlingsville. Knapp was not finished with his one-man construction boom, though. In 1825, he built a mill on Knapps' Bend. He inserted one run of Clarion River stone and opened a gristmill. For some time it was the only gristmill in Clover Township.

After the mill burned down in 1838, Knapp rebuilt it and operated it until 1844, when he sold the mill. That was fortunate for Knapp, because only three years later the mill was washed out in a flood.

The last mill that Knapp built was on the North Fork. In 1836, he built a mill about one mile upstream from the old Litch Mill dam. The mill operated under various owners until 1878, when it closed.

Knapp was also one of the first people elected to public office in Jefferson County. In a Pine Creek Township election in 1808, Knapp was elected as an auditor. In 1817, he was elected fence appraiser with a total of seven votes. In the election of 1829, Knapp was the big winner in the race for Rose Township supervisor with a total of thirty-nine votes.

He and Susan were members of the United Presbyterian Congregation of Jefferson. The church then stood southwest of Brookville on the north shore of the Red Bank Creek.

Moses Knapp died on May 14, 1859, at his home in Pine Creek Township at the age of seventy-six according to the death notice in the *Jeffersonian.*

The legend on his grave marker is not done in the standard block letters but rather in a coarse script. The stone, like the man, is very different from today's example.

## Tales from Puckerty Gap and Beyond

Jefferson County's early settlers found a cash crop waiting for them when they arrived. Deep, virgin forests stood waiting for the axe and saw. The settlers knew that the hardwoods were valuable, but they faced what seemed to be an insurmountable problem: geography. The solution was also at hand.

The county's streams emptied into the Allegheny River, which flowed to the market in Pittsburgh. Those early lumbermen knew that they could make rafts of their logs and float them to Pittsburgh, but the streams in the northern section of the county were small (often a person could walk across them without getting their ankles wet).

The innovative lumbermen decided to erect batten dams that would store the power of the spring rains until the water was high enough. The dams would then be opened, and the large log rafts would begin their journey to Pittsburgh, almost eighty miles downstream.

H.H. Kennedy of Brookville described his grandfather's experiences during the rafting era in Jefferson County. Kennedy said that when his grandfather arrived this section was a dense pine forest. As the neighborhood began to get settled, sawmills soon sprang up along the creeks in every direction to process lumber. The boards and planks that were sawed at the mills were made into great long rafts and run to Pittsburgh.

Kennedy said that a great amount of timber was cut into long logs. It was hewed into

> *square timber sticks and built into rafts held together with oak lash poles across the ends of each platform, held in place with oak bows over the poles, placed in holes bored in the sticks and fastened with oak pins driven in beside the bows with a pole axe. The platforms of the raft were coupled together in the same way by using the lash poles, bows and pins on the outside sticks on each side of them.*

Rafting on the Red Bank Creek.

"There was always some danger connected with rafting, for sometimes a raft would strike a rock on the bank in a short bend and you would have a wreck," wrote Kennedy.

The first sawmills were all run by water power and were called the old up-and-down mills. The logs were cut into boards and planks by a large straight saw (something like crosscut saws but straight on the edge—an apt description), fastened at each end in an upright position and worked up and down to cut through the logs. Kennedy said, "They worked slowly, and I have been told the man running the mill could start to cut through a log, go into the house and eat a lunch, drink a cup of coffee and get back to the mill before the saw would get a board off."

Historian Kate Scott noted the growth of the lumber industry:

> *In 1854 the lumber trade of the Red Bank Valley was estimated at over twenty million feet; on the North Fort there were twenty-two saws cutting ten million feet; on the Sandy Lick and its branches, twenty saws were cutting another ten million; while on Red Bank and Little Sandy, fifteen saws, cutting 3,500,000 raised the total estimate to 23,500,0000 feet. To this can be added at least five million shingles and about 1,200,000 feet linear, or square feet of timber, or about three million cubic feet.*

The sawmill in Brookville in 1898.

Running the rafts at least as far as the Allegheny was an event. Dr. William J. McKnight in his *History of the Jefferson County* recalled those days. "We usually had three floods on which to run this lumber—spring, June and fall. At these times rafts were plenty and people were scarce and, at time and tide wait came everybody had to turn out and assist to run the rafts."

Everyone got his feet wet. "The boy had to leave his school, the minister his pulpit, the doctor abandon his patients, the lawyer his briefs, the merchant his yardstick, the farmer his crops or seeding, and the editor his paper," wrote McKnight. "There was one great compensation in this, nearly everybody got to see Pittsburgh."

It was a rapid trip. "Running down the creek and gigging back was the business language of everybody at that time," said McKnight. "It took 12 hours to run a raft from the neighborhood of Brookville to the mouth of the Allegheny River, and ordinarily it required hard walking to reach home the next day."

All of this activity was limited to the area's creeks and rivers. At that time there were no railroads or even serviceable roads to handle the traffic. Soon,

The millpond in Brookville about 1898.

the streams became clogged with timber. Scott wrote that at the spring flood of 1869, 74 board rafts and 350 timber rafts were run out of Red Bank by Jefferson County lumbermen, containing over 2,500,000 feet of boards and 600,000 square feet of timber.

In 1872, 917 timber rafts and 570 board rafts were run out of the Red Bank from the waters of Sandy Lick, North Fork, Little Sandy and Red Bank. The timber rafts from the three former streams averaged 16,000 feet per raft and those from Little Sandy, 1,000 feet; the board rafts ran from 25,000 to 50,000, making a total run for the year of 1,500,000 feet of square timber and 20 million feet of boards. These comprised shipments of 150 individuals and firms, averaging from 1 to 100 rafts each.

Acts were passed in the Pennsylvania legislature declaring the principal streams as highways. The next step was to form navigation companies. On May 17, 1854, the legislature approved the creation of the Red Bank Navigation Company. Thomas K. Litch, Thomas Reynolds, Daniel Smith, Darius Carrier and Patrick Kerr were appointed commissioners to carry out the provisions of the act.

The third section of the act gave the company power to clean and clear the Red Bank, Sandy Lick and North Fork from all rocks, bars and other obstructions; to erect dams and locks; to bracket and regulate all dams now erected; to regulate the chutes of dames; to control the waters for purposes of navigation; and to levy tolls not exceeding one and one-quarter cents for each and every five miles of improved creek, per thousand feet of boards or other sawed stuff, for every foot, linear measure of square or other timber. These tolls were to be collected at the mouth of the Red Bank or at such points as were deemed necessary.

Under the provisions of this act, the streams were greatly improved, and during the first three years the tolls collected amounted to over three thousand dollars, the greater part of which was expended to improve channels.

The lumber barons also had another reason of wanting power to control the waters. Every year, they lost money when some of their logs were appropriated by what was termed "Algerines." The term referred to the infamous Barbary Coast pirates, and like their North African brethren, these pirates stole any logs that floated downstream without proper guard. With

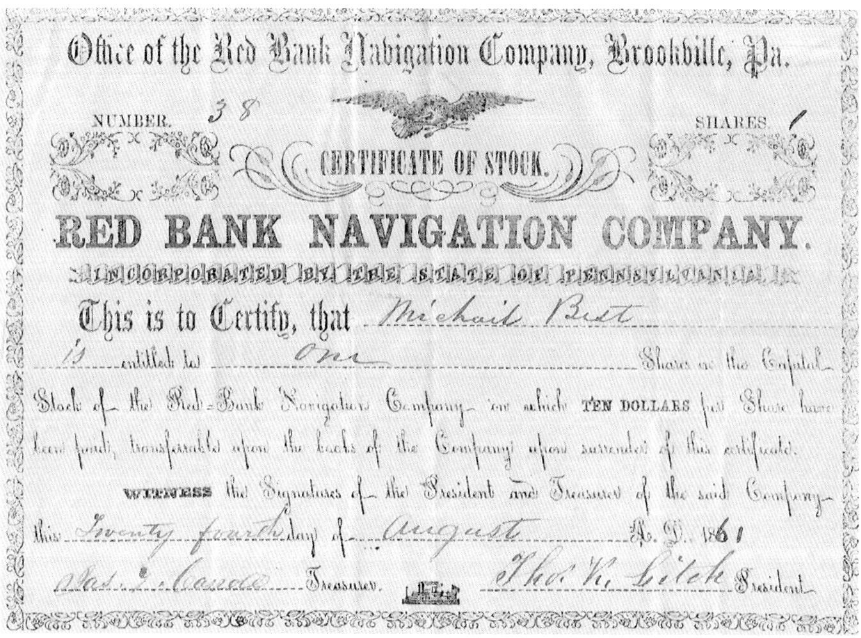

Office of the Red Bank Navigation Company, Brookville, Pa.

NUMBER. 38 SHARES. 1

CERTIFICATE OF STOCK.

RED BANK NAVIGATION COMPANY.

INCORPORATED BY THE STATE OF PENNSYLVANIA.

This is to Certify, that Michael Best is entitled to One Shares in the Capital Stock of the Red Bank Navigation Company on which TEN DOLLARS per Share have been paid, transferable upon the books of the Company upon surrender of this certificate.

WITNESS the Signatures of the President and Treasurer of the said Company this Twenty fourth day of August A. D. 1861

[illegible] Treasurer. President

Stock certificate No. 38 in the Red Bank Navigation Company, issued to Michael Best, August 24, 1861.

power invested in them, the lumber barons wasted little time in clearing the rivers of natural and human obstructions.

The once vast forests of the region were ravaged by the early lumbermen. Soon, it became apparent that the lumber boon was about to go bust. In her 1888 *History of Jefferson County*, Scott saw the writing on the wall. "But the pristine glory of Red Bank has departed: The mighty monarchs of the forest that clothed the banks of it and its tributaries have been laid low. The lumber trade of Jefferson County in a few years will be a thing of the past. The pine timber, in the handling of which large fortunes were accumulated, and which was for so long the staple products of the county, will soon be cut away."

Scott was correct. The county's first lumbering boom was almost over. On June 20, 1905, Alfred Truman wrote of the closing of the last sawmill in Brookville. "At five minutes before nine o'clock in the morning, I watched the sawing of the last log that will ever be cut into boards on the Cook sawmill in Brookville. The old mill is dead. We will never hear its noise again," he said. "We have lumbered as nations war, as if the only object was destruction."

In Jefferson County today, the lumber industry has returned. Much of the forest has regrown through reforestation, and once again saws can be heard in the woods. A small section of that original virgin forest has been preserved and is now a part of the Cook Forest State Park—saved, ironically, by a lumberman.

## Guarding the Frontier

When Jefferson County was settled around 1800, there were still a few Native Americans in the area. As the numbers of white settlers increased, the numbers of the original inhabitants decreased. That did not mean that the settlers were free from any threat to their safety. Just to the north was the British dominion of Canada, the scene of conflict during the Revolution. In the War of 1812, the Great Lakes became the cockpit of the fighting. British raids into New York were not unknown, and with the British often came Indian allies.

The people of Jefferson County had a compelling reason to comply with the Pennsylvania militia law. A resolution adopted by the Pennsylvania Military Convention in 1856 stated, "Believing that when there is a well organized citizen soldiery there is no need for a standing army," the Brookville Guards, Jefferson County's original militia unit, was formed.

According to the original roll book of the company, Amos Mercer, the brigade inspector, organized the Brookville Guards on Friday, May 24, 1844. The thin volume details the constitution of the Guards, its bylaws and a roll of the men present for drill. The record becomes less clear as the years progressed, but entries were made in the book for fifteen years, up until 1859.

Jefferson County was barely over a decade old and still very much a frontier community. The militia movement of the day was born out of the belief that a citizen force could be mustered to defend the nation. That mirage continued until the start of the Civil War.

Those early militiamen set some noble goals for themselves. Under the militia law of Pennsylvania, the Guards could make rules and regulations members deemed "proper" for the good of the order. One important provision was added: the rules had to be in accordance with the laws of the state and the nation.

Each applicant for membership was reviewed and accepted by a vote of the company. Each successful candidate had to pay twenty-five cents into the treasury. Each man was also responsible for his own equipment.

The uniforms were unique, even by the standards of the day. A blue "drilling coatee" trimmed in red was worn over white "drilling pants" trimmed with a black stripe down the outside seam. A black velvet cap with a "glazed top" was tipped with an ostrich plume that started at the left side and ran across to the right-hand side.

In addition, each man had to have a white belt two inches wide. Not wearing a belt or wearing a belt too wide led to a fine of six and one-quarter cents per day.

The company's cadre consisted of one captain, one first lieutenant, one second lieutenant and a first sergeant. The company would meet four days each year for training: the first Monday in May, the Fourth of July, the tenth day of September and one day selected by the company.

Unless an excuse was presented, the soldiers could be fined for being absent. The fine for commissioned officers was two dollars, noncommissioned officers and privates, one dollar each.

If a soldier turned out for parade in an intoxicated state, he would be publically reprimanded, and a second offense could lead to a fifty-cent fine. A third offense would mean dismissal from the company "without the privilege of rejoining the same."

Elected as captain was Evans R. Brady, Andrew Craig as first lieutenant, James Ames as second lieutenant and John Hastings as first sergeant.

Seventy-six names are listed on the rolls. Many of those names are familiar to county residents today: Templeton, Fullerton, Clark, Reed, Steele, Christie, McManigle, Nolf, Rankin, Campbell, Wilson, Huffman, Fogle, Darrah, Larimer, McCreight and Dowling.

On June 28, the company paraded with forty-five privates, and a requisition was made to the commonwealth for fifty muskets, fifty cartridge boxes, fifty bayonets and fifty bayonet scabbards. In September, fifty knapsacks were requisitioned along with tents.

The muskets were kept in an armory in Brookville and taken out only for drill. It appears that when the company was first formed the full fifty muskets were needed at any one drill. In 1847, however, only thirty-one muskets were needed.

The book does not detail any drills and yields no information until the final entries in 1859. On September 13, three men—James Averill, John Thompson and James Anderson—were each paid fifty cents on a "refunding order."

The Brookville Guards did not see any active service, but many of its men served their country during the Civil War in the new volunteer regiments.

Like the National Guard of today, the early militiamen stood ready to respond to their country's call.

## THE PIONEER RESURRECTION

The door to the icehouse was opened just a crack, just enough for fifteen-year-old Willie Smith to peek inside. What he saw inside the icehouse set off a wave of terror and panic in Brookville.

Inside, lying on the blocks of river ice, was the dismembered body of a man. Young Smith ran screaming from the icehouse, a block behind the Jefferson County Courthouse. Soon a curious crowd converged on the icehouse at the corner of Coal Alley and Pickering Street.

The man's body, or what was left of it, was displayed spread eagle with a board behind his head. The corpse had been skinned and several organs removed. Clearly foul play was afoot on that cold Sunday morning, November 8, 1857. But what ghouls could have perpetrated such a deed? And who was the poor unfortunate who had been the victim of this butchery?

Henry R. Fullerton examined the corpse and found a clue: a bit of curly hair that may have belonged to a recently deceased black man from Pine Creek Township, Henry Southerland.

Dr. William J. McKnight.
*Courtesy of the Jefferson County Historical Society.*

Southerland was described as a "stout, perfect specimen of physical manhood." He had contracted a fever in October and had died at the age of thirty years. Southerland had died about ten days before and was buried in the old Brookville Cemetery at the summit of Pickering Street.

When Fullerton announced his discovery, a mob armed with tools and led by Cyrus Butler, Fullerton and Richard Arthur climbed the hill and went to Southerland's grave. After turning a few shovelfuls of dirt, a slipper was found and, a bit deeper, its mate. The coffin was found but it was empty. Only the clothes, obviously torn off the body, remained in the wooden box.

Butler, who was described as a "gruff old man" stated flatly, "Men these days will do anything for money." That thin premise was held to be true, and it was believed that Southerland's skin was being tanned for commercial purposes by those who had disturbed his eternal rest.

A coroner's inquest was called that very day, and the twelve men were summoned to examine the body that was still in the icehouse. Taking the grisly tour were newspaper editor Evans R. Brady, J.J.Y. Thompson, Andrew Craig, John Boucher, Levi Dodd, Christopher Smathers, Henry Fullerton, G.W. Andrews, S.C. Arthurs, John Carroll, John Ramsey and Daniel Smith. The panel concluded that the body was indeed that of Henry Southerland. They also concluded that the actors were unknown. Their verdict was not popular in the community.

Suspicion fell upon the Masons—"It was the custom then to charge all unpopular verdicts on the Masons." The town was in a panic. If graves could be defiled, anything was possible "for money."

Southerland's corpse was removed from the icehouse in a rude fashion. A rope was tied about his neck, and he was drug out of the building and into the street, where his coffin awaited. (His grave cannot be found in the old cemetery today.)

Meanwhile, the search for the ghouls brought "stupidity and prejudice" to the fore. Two innocent black men living in Pine Creek Township were hauled into Brookville to face the charges. It soon became evident, however, that they were innocent.

The uncertainty remained among the citizens, and several graves of the recently departed were opened just to be certain that they were right where they were supposed to be. A citizens' guard was placed around the cemetery to prevent any further intrusions.

Brady, who had seen the corpse as a member of the coroner's panel, ventured a theory on the crime. "It is now believed by every person that the body was placed in the ice house for dissection," he said.

Amor A. McKnight, a young attorney in Brookville, had heard some rather disconcerting rumors. He had been told by his mother that his brother, Dr. William J. McKnight, had been one of the perpetrators who had dug up Southerland.

As an officer of the court, Amor did his duty and "made information" against his brother to Squire Smith. The doctor was arrested along with the appropriately named Kennedy L. Blood, a local druggist. Grave robbing and dissection of a human being, even for medical study, was illegal in Pennsylvania.

Dr. McKnight entered a guilty plea and paid a twenty-five-dollar fine. Dr. McKnight was the only person convicted, but he did not act alone.

It was not until all of the other "ghouls" had departed this earth that Dr. McKnight revealed the truth about what had become known as the pioneer resurrection. McKnight was one of seven men involved in the late-night activities at the cemetery.

In his *History of Jefferson County*, McKnight wrote that Doctors J.G. Simmons, John and Hugh Dowling and A.P. Heichhold and friends K.L. Blood and Augustus Bell took the hike up the hill to the cemetery fortified with a little whiskey.

Having disinterred the body, the doctors did not seem to possess a clear plan, which may have been the result of the whiskey. In any event, they took Southerland's body to the home of Mrs. Ada Means and placed it in a small bedroom. She became understandably nervous, and the conspirators had to move the body again. They wanted to protect Dr. William Clarke, who lived nearby, so the somewhat inebriated party placed Southerland's body in a coffee sack and stuffed him under a neighbor's front porch. Southerland lay there in uneasy rest until his remains were taken to the icehouse for the pioneer anatomy class.

The body of Henry Southerland was stashed under the front porch of this Main Street house.

All of the doctors, including McKnight, went on to distinguished careers, and Southerland was returned to his grave, never to rise again. Years later, when Dr. McKnight was serving in the Pennsylvania legislature, he wrote legislation that was adopted into law allowing the dissection of bodies for medical study.

## The Underground Railroad Uncovered

At the bottom of a set of cellar stairs is a door. It is very unremarkable except for its age. The door has been guarding a secret for over one hundred years in the house on Pickering Street. This seemingly unremarkable portal was viewed as the door to freedom by hundreds of runaway slaves in the early 1800s. Behind that door was welcome relief for the fugitives on their long trek to Canada. The door guarded a way station of the Underground Railroad in Brookville.

On entering the door, one must turn to the right or left. Down the right side is a thin corridor leading to a very small room, just large enough for two

Student volunteer Steve Snell helps to excavate the tunnel in the Underground Railroad station. The tunnel led from the well house to the room in which escaped slaves rested.

or three persons. Although some changes have taken place in the original configuration, it is not difficult to see the basic outline.

An excellent description of the space is available through a small article in a turn-of-the-century newspaper. Dr. C.M. Matson, who occupied the house in 1902, was making repairs to the property and discovered the entry, a passageway leading to the cellar, "nearly bricked up, about two feet wide and three to four feet high…This passageway led to a room under the ground, outside the building about eight feet square." Dr. Matson speculated at that time that the room was probably the work of Judge Elijah Heath, an early abolitionist. In all probability, the doctor's guess was correct.

Heath was not the only area resident involved with the underground network, but he was the most prominent. He was a most outspoken advocate of immediate abolition and also a man of action, a combination that nearly ruined him.

Volunteer Evie Johnson works in the well at the Underground Railroad site under the direction of Carnegie Museum Field Archaeologist Ken Burkett.

It would seem that in 1834 two fugitives were captured and brought to the newly erected Jefferson County Jail to be held overnight. The judge was outraged. The fugitives would probably have met with a gruesome fate if they had been returned to their "rightful owners." The judge was determined to help the men escape.

This was no easy matter, for the new jail was a two-story brick building that had just been completed the year before. Not only were the prisoners lodged on the second floor of the building, but the sheriff, Thomas McKee, also lived in the building.

Undaunted, the good judge conveyed to the runaways, through the jailor, Arad Pearsall, implements for filing off the lock of their cell. By morning the inmates were gone, probably into hiding and perhaps into the cellar on Pickering Street, only a block from the jail. The judge did not escape so easily.

Eventually, he was convicted of violating the Fugitive Slave Act and was fined the enormous sum of $2,000. The judge managed to frustrate his prosecutors by conveying his property to others until he could "compromise the case."

The home of Judge Elijah Heath and a refuge for escaped slaves.

Heath was only one of many who had taken up the cause. The long, slow passage from the South required many hands. In Jefferson County, the route came up from Indiana County and exited at the Clarion River near Clarington. In Punxsutawney, James Minish was the station master. He would relay the fugitives to Isaac Carmalt down in Clayville, who would lead them to the Reverend Christopher Fogle in Troy (Summerville) and on to Pearsall, Heath and James Steadman in Brookville. The final link in the long line was the home of William Coon in Clarington. Coon had the job of ferrying the fugitives across the Clarion River.

The work was dangerous for both the slave and the station master. Several accounts survive of slaves taking to the woods to avoid capture by the slave hunters. The work went on, however, and generally, at least in this area, with an official blind eye.

Usually slaves moving in twos or threes did not attract attention, but an early Brookville paper reported in an editorial fashion that "25 fugitive slaves passed through Brookville Monday morning on their way to Canada." Hardly a well-kept secret.

The work of early abolitionists or gradualists ceased with the opening of the Civil War. But in those years, it is estimated that at least 1,500 fugitives each year found their way to freedom on the Underground Railroad. The small room, forgotten for so many years, is the only authenticated way station left in Brookville. More important than the small space is the idea, a lesson as relevant today as it was when the small room was scooped out of the earth, that no man should be forced to live in another's chains.

## Slyhoff's Grave

In the early days of Jefferson County, there lived a man who placed money above all else. Richard Slyhoff lived north of Brookville around the Sigel area in the 1850s and 1860s. He was one of those hardy pioneers who carved out a living from the land, but unlike many of those early residents, he had a heart as hard as flint.

Slyhoff was never accused of being generous and was never known to darken the door of any church on anything like a regular basis. There are few existing records of his dealings, but they must have sharp indeed, for his reputation survives today. His dark heart has become the stuff of a rural legend. The tale grew larger and larger after his death, and it became

The grave of Richard Slyhoff.

popular for many years to have a picnic at Slyhoff's Grave. It was at these gatherings that the oral tale of Richard Slyhoff was finally taken down and preserved. It is a story of good and evil, and how evil will be punished… eventually.

Slyhoff was said to be an ungodly man, having lived far from the straight and narrow. As he aged, he began to fear what may be in store for him in the next world. He came to believe that the devil would surely get him when he died. Many of his business associates probably believed that the devil already possessed Slyhoff.

Slyhoff, always looking for the angle, concocted what he came to believe was a foolproof way of evading eternal justice.

It is said that Slyhoff was familiar with all the country around Brookville and knew about a certain large rock that leaned far over, at an angle of approximately forty-five degrees. It leaned so far over that it looked as if the slightest tremor of the earth would cause it to fall. That is exactly what Slyhoff was looking for.

In the fullness of his years, Slyhoff came to that time where he was about to die. He felt the cold hands reaching out for his soul, and that is when he put his escape plan into action. He had conceived the idea that if he were buried beneath this leaning rock he would be safe from the devil when the Judgment Day arrived. He reasoned that as the earth trembled and the dead came forth from their graves, the leaning rock would shake and fall over on his grave, completely and forever burying him and separating him from the devil for all time.

According to his wish, he was buried beneath the leaning rock. This was no easy task. He wanted to be certain that his grave would lay safely out of the reach of the devil so he paid the gravediggers to scrape out what he hoped would be his final resting place far under the leaning rock. The men had to get on their hands and knees under the rock in order to scoop out the earth, and even then they were constantly bumping their heads. It is doubtful that the gravediggers had any kind words to say over Slyhoff's grave. Their work was not done, however. In order to get the coffin placed in its final resting place, it was necessary to slide it under the rock and then let it down with ropes held by men a short distance from the rock. Finally the grave was dug and the late Slyhoff was laid to his eternal rest, or so he thought.

The grave was almost completely hidden by the leaning rock. When the grave marker was placed, it was necessary to put the small footstone under the rock (presumably at Slyhoff's feet) and the head stone placed at the outer edge of the rock. The inscription was carved on the side away from the grave.

That is where the story should have ended, but it was only beginning.

Since the time Slyhoff was buried in 1867, the rock has moved! There have been no local earthquakes, no floods and no man-made movements, but the rock has moved and not in the direction that Slyhoff had anticipated. Whether by supernatural forces or by the forces of nature, no one knows, but the fact remains that the rock has drawn steadily away from the grave. Today, the rock does not lean toward the grave at all but stands perpendicular or even leans a little away from the grave!

This is the legend of Slyhoff's grave, a man who tried to cheat what fate waits.

## KATE SCOTT, A PIONEERING WOMAN

The small tombstone in the Brookville Cemetery reads simply:

*Kate Scott, Army Nurse, Authoress, 1837–1911*

Those bland lines barely touch on the life of one of Jefferson County's most renowned citizens. In her lifetime, Kate Scott was a printer, editor, writer, postmistress, nurse and historian. This may sound like a resume for a modern woman, but Scott lived during the Victorian age, when women were seldom allowed careers outside the home.

Kate Scott was born in Ebensburg, the oldest of five children born to John and Hannah Scott. She received a formal education at the Blairsville Seminary, but her true education began when she worked at the side of her father, the publisher and editor of the *Brookville Republican*. In a front-page tribute published at the time of her death, her career with the newspaper was cited. Not only did she write copy and edit stories, but she also performed the taxing job of "sticking type." It would have been her responsibility to place each letter of lead type into a sliding stick, which would then be placed in line for use on the printing press. Not only was it small type, but it all had to be done backward.

Kate Scott grew up in the charged political atmosphere of the 1850s. The *Republican* was the local mouthpiece for the fledgling political party and started printing just in time for the election of 1856. Democrat James Buchannan, a Pennsylvanian, won the presidency but not the hearts of the people. In 1860, the fractured Democratic Party could not settle on a single candidate, opening the door for Republican Abraham Lincoln to become the first president from that party.

During this period, columns appearing in the *Republican* bore the signature KMS for Kate M. Scott. She was by far the earliest female reporter not only in this area but possibly in the nation.

For a time she taught school, but her first love was always writing. That career was rudely interrupted by the outbreak of the Civil War. As a woman, Scott could not join the army, but she wanted to serve. She saw her opportunity when the call went out for nurses.

Under the system of the day, each regiment was authorized to recruit its own nurses. Colonel Amor A. McKnight issued a call for nurses for the 105$^{th}$ Regiment of Pennsylvania Volunteers, who were also known as the Wild Cat Regiment.

Kate Scott as a nurse during the Civil War. *Courtesy of Ken Burkett.*

Scott, Lydia Myers, Ellen Guffy, Mary Allen and Mary Fryer volunteered and soon found themselves at Camp Jameson near Washington, D.C. The camp proved to be an unhealthy place, and the troops suffered from fever, pneumonia and smallpox.

The Brookville "nurses" had practically no training. The same could be said for their male counterparts. Scott said that their purpose was "to aid the recovery of the many who were stricken down by disease." Often they had nothing but home remedies with which to work.

The nurses were not immune to the sickness in the camp. Twice in the first winter of the war, the 105th was quarantined for smallpox. Ellen Guffy contracted the disease, and Scott stayed with her friend, risking infection herself until Guffy recovered. The two women were quarantined a second time, but this time the enemy was typhoid fever.

These women were pioneers in the nursing field when it was a social taboo for women to work with men in that capacity. Dorothea Dix, the head of the federal nursing corps, made it clear that she did not want attractive women in her organization who may be more interested in snaring a husband than caring for the wounded. Her service as a nurse marked Scott and the others as true pioneers in nursing.

The volunteer nurses were sent home in 1862 when the army moved south. Her experiences with the soldiers stayed with Scott for the rest of her life. Long after the war, she wrote the regimental history of the 105$^{th}$, the only period woman to write such a history. She was inducted into the regiment's reunion organization as an honorary member. Scott served as the secretary for the organization from 1879 to 1891. That position gave Kate Scott the distinction of being one of the first women to be recognized by a veteran's organization.

Returning to Brookville, Scott resumed her duties with the newspaper and filled her father's shoes as the editor when he was absent. Scott's newspaper was perceived as being loyal to the administration and was well received during the war years. It was also popular among the soldiers, who often wrote long, descriptive letters to the *Republican*. Those letters were printed without any censorship, which was a great boon for future historians, including Kate Scott.

Following the success of *The History of the 105$^{th}$ Pennsylvania*, published in 1877, Scott set about on her most ambitious work, a history of Jefferson County. In 1888, she completed the first history of the county. The work stands the test of time and is written in a plain style typical of Scott's writing. The work took two years to complete, and for her effort, Scott received nine hundred dollars.

Her energies were not confined to writing. This remarkable woman was active in the Independent Order of Good Templars, a temperance organization, where she served as the worth deputy marshal. It was her work with the Women's Relief Corps (WRC) that was her passion. She took the lead in the purchase of the old Longview Hotel in Brookville and its conversion into a home for old soldiers and their wives. Her letters written at the time scold the national and state WRC for not moving more quickly on the purchase of the hotel. She was elected secretary of the Pennsylvania WRC for several years. The Pennsylvania Memorial Home was a landmark in Brookville for many years and a testament to the tenacity of one very determined woman.

Scott and her brother, John, operated the Punxsutawney Plain Dealer for two years but returned to Brookville in 1870. She worked in the Brookville Post Office with her father and then with two other postmasters before being appointed as Brookville's first female postmistress in 1890. Her appointment was disputed and led to an election, which she won handily.

Her last literary effort was a biographical booklet on the Civil War army nurses. It is the only such collection compiled by a woman who had served in that capacity.

A member of the National Association of Army Nurses, Scott used her not inconsiderable influence (and pen) to lobby for a pension for the aged women. In a letter written to her co-lobby, Scott said, "Now about this pension business that has nearly killed us both, well it is my last try for pensions for our old nurses." The signature on the letter was frail, but the spirit was still strong. The pension, twelve dollars per month, was granted after Scott died. Her last try was good enough.

Kate Scott died at her Jefferson Street home in Brookville at 6:30 p.m. on a Saturday evening, April 15, 1911. She was seventy-four years of age. It was reported that she was surrounded by family and friends when she passed away. At her funeral, a detail from the Evans R. Brady Post of the Grand Army of the Republic served as an honor guard.

So passed one of Jefferson County's most noted citizens. In the chronicles of Jefferson County written by Kate Scott and others, one chapter is missing—a chapter on Kate Scott, a true pioneer.

## The Curious Case of Kate Scott

Kate M. Scott was indeed an influential woman in Victorian Brookville. Her service during the Civil War as a volunteer nurse and her support of veterans made her a revered figure. That was the public side of the county's first historian, but there exists a curious document that sheds a different light on this complex woman. The document is in the collection of the Cunningham Memorial Library, in Terre Haute, Indiana, and is available online.

The document is a sworn statement given by a woman claiming to be "Kate M. Scott of 295 Jefferson Street, Brookville, Commonwealth of Pennsylvania and late of the Army Nurses during the War of the Rebellion associated with the 105th Regiment Pennsylvania Volunteers."

Kate Scott later in life.

The statement is dated the twenty-seventh day of October, 1910, and recorded at 2317 Thirteenth Street, Washington, D.C., the northwest section, and made to Osborn Hamlin Oldroyd, Esquire.

The biographical comments made in the statement match the known facts of Scott's family and early life. It was at the outbreak of the War of the Rebellion that her life changed.

The Scott in this statement said, "I was a completely innocent and naïve young lady from a small country town and lacking the ability to cope with the fast talking men of the large cities. I was graceful enough in my home but felt terribly insecure when I left."

When the war began, Scott was twenty-four years old and was being courted by a young man from Clarion. Her beau was caught up in the fervor of the times and immediately joined a regiment. She said, "I could go with him and I readily became determined to become a nurse with the troops.

I immediately wrote a letter to the commander of the military district and within several weeks received instructions on how I should apply."

Scott did join the 105th Regiment as a nurse and followed them to Washington, D.C.

In the statement, Scott wrote of her struggle to overcome the jumbled government bureaucracy. After reaching Harrisburg, she found no travel money waiting for her and went to work sewing uniforms to raise the sixteen-dollar train fare for the journey to Washington.

She finally arrived in Washington on November 26 but still had to make the trip to Camp Jamison. The provost marshal, accustomed to women of a certain character visiting the troops, refused to let her cross the river. Scott said that she resorted to subterfuge, obtained some men's clothing and walked to Camp Jamison. Even then a sentry stopped her, thinking she was a spy. She saw Colonel Amor A. McKnight, a Brookville attorney, and "ran to him, pulled off my hat, and told him who I was." She was now a nurse with the troops.

Unlike her public demeanor, the Kate Scott of this statement revealed army indifference, horrible conditions and a frustration not seen in any of her other writing. "It was not long before I was put to work." She said she arrived in the camp during an epidemic and that she worked every day for sixteen to twenty hours per day until January 5. Scott was critical of the hospital at Camp Jamison, "if indeed it could be called a hospital." It was a clapboard building with "cracks in the floor and walls so that the cold wind blew through and the fine snow even blew in little piles."

In the statement, Scott said the most discouraging thing was the attitude of the officers of the camp. "I had thought that we would be looked upon as some kind of angel of mercy but such was not the case. We were treated much like servants and camp followers and we were constantly being approached for illicit propositions. The surgeons were little better and there were several who were especially repulsive in their manners, or rather, lack of manners." Although she would not "engage in name calling," there was a major in the medical service who was "constantly getting me into positions where he could put his hands on me and he did the same for the other two nurses who were there."

The nurses fared better with the enlisted men. "The beastly behavior of the men was generally found in the officers and very much less in the enlisted men. There were hospital stewards there who respected us and treated us with kindness and courtesy. Had it not been for them, I would not have stayed a week," she wrote.

Her "true love" was now a captain in the regiment, but there was little time to see him. Discouraged by her experiences, Scott decided that when the army left Camp Jamison she would find a job in Washington or return to Brookville.

When the first of March came, she left the camp and moved into a boardinghouse on Tenth Street in Washington. Friends of Scott, Mr. and Mrs. Judson Weaver, had come to Washington, and she soon moved in with them. During this period Scott became aware of the Washington social life. She said she attended military balls with the Weavers, and at one of these social functions she met the actor John Wilkes Booth. She wrote, "We danced together and I found him extremely attractive. Very soon thereafter he called on me at the Weavers and we began to keep company. I attended social functions with him and he visited me often at the Weavers. I knew that he was also keeping company with at least one other young lady but I did not fear but what I could hold my own with the competition. How naive I was."

She stated that she did not know then that Booth was married or "I should not have gone out with him."

In June, she returned to Brookville and spent the summer busy with the chores "which were to be done in a home with no mother."

That fall, her cousins, who were sea captains, visited Brookville to hunt birds. They also brought a guest: John Wilkes Booth. She said she was "not so sure that I was glad to see Mr. Booth."

"He and I had seen too much of each other when I was in Washington and I had come to decide that I could not capture the heart of Mr. Booth for I did not believe that he really had a heart," she wrote. "He was such a gentleman and such a scoundrel at the same time. I really cared for him but I knew that I could never receive from him the love that I longed so for."

Booth was known to have been investing in oil speculations with Winston Weaver in Oil City and Meadville. Booth spent much of time in those places, but "he returned by way of Brookville." Scott said that Booth had business with her seafaring cousins, John Evan Scott and John Celestina. She said both were involved with blockade running, but that was not known to her at the time.

During the visit, Scott said that Robby Bernard, a boy from Brookville who was now a government detective, came to Brookville and dropped in for a visit. He asked her questions about her cousins and was "very suspicious of them."

Her relationship with Booth continued during the next year, when he would drop by to see her on his trip to or from Meadville and he would spend the night with the family. It is curious that there is no mention of a visit by the renowned actor in any of the Brookville newspapers, including the Scott family's *Brookville Republican*.

Scott said that she "soon came to look on these visits with great expectations and I soon found that I was much too fond of Mr. Booth than I should be for my own good." Her relationship with Booth soon reached the distant ears of her "true love," and he wrote her a scorching letter. The result was that he married another woman. Soon after he married, he died in battle.

Scott said that she read about the marriage in the newspaper on the sixth of February, a Saturday. That night, John Wilkes Booth came to the Scott house and planned to spend the night. What happened next, Scott said, was "a reaction to my terrible hurt and disappointment that caused me to do the things that I did." She went with him to Meadville and returned to Washington with him. She spent the next month with the Weavers in Washington and returned to Brookville the middle of March.

Scott said that she had a daughter who was born in Indianapolis, Indiana, on December 8, 1865. "To this day I have never told anyone who the father was nor the circumstances of her birth," she said. "While you may know some of the facts you do not know them all nor shall you, nor shall anyone else. Some things are so sacred as to be unmentionable."

Scott said that she received payments "made to me and my daughter" by the law firm of Weaver and Weaver. The payments stopped in 1886, when her daughter reached her majority. Her daughter received the residue of the annuity. "She is happily married and is fully aware of all there is to know. I will not reveal her identity," Scott said in her statement.

Scott was shocked when the details of President Lincoln's assassination became known. "I could not believe that Booth had been involved and yet, I realized that he had been," she wrote. "He was such a calm and loving person but he believed so deeply in the cause of peace and freedom. Then there was the story of his death and I felt so sorry that so great a talent had been wasted."

However, Scott said that history had the story of Booth's death all wrong. In July, she received a letter in "handwriting that was most unmistakably his," asking her to see Winston Weaver and "get from him an envelope which had been left with him a number of months before." She was instructed to meet him at the Scott farm on September 15. The note was signed "John Byron Wilkes."

Booth appeared without his moustache, and his appearance was "otherwise changed so that he looked completely different." When she expressed concern for his safety, he told her that he was "to the entire world, dead and buried and that no one would recognize him." He told Scott that he had sent his valet and another man from Harrisburg on to New York while he made his way to Brookville, from where he would go on to Niagara Falls and cross into Canada.

Scott said that Booth's leg was "almost well and he walked with only a slight favoring of the left foot. He rode a horse quite well with no problems of mounting or dismounting."

The couple spent the rest of the week at the farm, and she "begged him to take me with him." Booth told her that he could not but that he would "send for me later." Booth told her he had made arrangements to go to India, where he could live in peace. He had ample funds in the Bank of England, and his financial future was assured. Booth told her that he would meet her cousin Captain John Scott in Canada and that he would go to India on his ship.

Her other cousin, John Celestina, had been arrested as having taken part in the conspiracy, but he had been released in July and had left the country. She said both John Scott and John Celestina had "stood by with their ships to take Booth and his party out of the country."

The Scott statement claimed that she received several letters from Booth after he arrived in England and several more after he was in India. She also claims that Booth died in the early 1880s. None of these letters is known to have survived.

Booth also related details of his escape after the assassination at Ford's Theatre. Unlike the accepted version of the story, which had Booth cornered and killed at a farm near Fredericksburg, Virginia, Scott claims that when Booth escaped from Washington he had made his way to a cavern in Green County, where he spent a week or so. Booth told her he then went to a farm owned by Lewis Pence in Rockingham County, Virginia, where he had recovered further. He said he had then been taken by Pence to his farm in Harpers Ferry, where he had stayed for some time before heading for Canada.

Nothing of this story has been corroborated by historians.

The final section of the statement shows a very different side of Kate Scott. "I to this day believe that the War of the Rebellion was fought for purely political purposes and for the financial gain of persons who found it good for business. Ways of peacefully settling the dispute could have been found," she said.

She also wrote that she had been a member of an organization known as the Order of the Tear, "an organization devoted to the ending of war and fighting and orderly resistance to the draft." This statement has also not been documented.

The statement also vented her frustration at being a second-class citizen:

> *I do not believe that women exist for the pleasure of men but rather that men and women exist for the mutual pleasure of them both. I find the overbearing and self-justifying attitude of most men disgusting and crude. If that makes me a woman's rights man then so be it. The day must surely come when women will vote, hold political office, and enjoy all the freedoms which men today enjoy. No longer will she be looked upon as a child-bearing machine produced for the service and pleasure of men.*

This statement may explain why she never married.

Her friends would also have been surprised by her next statement:

> *We who resisted the draft did not do it as traitors to our country but rather as patriots to a new and peaceful country. The government looked upon us, even though they did not know who we were in most instances, as "Copperhead traitors" but we were nothing of the sort. The draft resistance was in both the North and the South and was based on good humanitarian motives.*

The statement was signed by Kate M. Scott (born Mary Katherine Scott). She died a year later. The statement has been used in several published works but has been dismissed by mainstream historians. The questions remain unanswered but certainly add another element to the story of Kate Scott.

## The High Cost of Black Gold

In 1916, there were sixty-nine mines in operation in Jefferson, Clearfield, Elk, Clarion, Clinton and Cameron Counties, producing 4,784,817 tons of coal. That coal was not mined without a price. In that twelve-month period, there were six fatalities below ground, which according to Dr. William J. McKnight's history of Jefferson County was a fortunate year "as regards the

The Daugherty Mine.

loss of life" and serious injuries inside the mines. "A greater tonnage of coal was mined per life lost for the year than for any other period in the history of the district," said McKnight.

In the early years of the twentieth century, when deep mining was common in the area, fatalities were almost a weekly occurrence. It was a dangerous business. Rock falls, explosions from gases and blasting accidents would maim or kill miners.

Area newspapers were filled with industrial accidents. Men died on the railroad, in lumber mills and in the mines. Dr. McKnight notes the difference between mining fatalities below and above ground. Working above ground could be just as deadly.

In September 1901, two men were killed in the mines at Big Soldier. According to the *Jeffersonian Democrat*, Richard Jennings of Reynoldsville and an unnamed "Polander" were working at the tipple of the R&P coal mine when nine mine cars derailed, crushing Jennings's skull. The "Polander" was caught between the cars and crushed.

In November 1901, a young man named Norman Fike died while he was working in a new shaft near Sykesville. According to the *Falls Creek Herald*,

The Cascade Mine.

the accident occurred when a car of coal was being hauled up the shaft. As the car neared the top of the shaft, the machinery broke, sending the car, its contents and the timber beams supporting the apparatus down the shaft. A piece of timber struck Fike in the head, killing him instantly.

Some of the accidents did not even take place near a mine but rather in industries that supplied the mines. Black powder was a necessary commodity in the mines. The highly volatile powder was used to blast the rock walls and enlarge the shafts. The Punxsutawney Powder Company had been in operation for only six months when an explosion tore the plant apart in April 1902. Three men were working in the plant at the time—Clark Simpson, Joseph Weiss and Orvil Bargerstock. All three men died instantly when 1,500 pounds of black powder ignited. Weiss's body was torn into fragments, and the other two were "mangled beyond recognition," according to local newspapers.

In April 1903, four miners working the London mine near DuBois were killed when a section of the roof collapsed on them. George Truax of DuBois, Edward Fye and Earl Waggett of "the Patch" near Falls Creek and William Phillips of Rochester mines were killed and two other men were seriously injured when a "slip" in the mine roof caused the collapse. Local newspapers said that the four men were buried under an "awful weight."

The Cascade Mine and coke works.

In the same month, another miner was killed while "robbing pillars" in the Rochester mine near DuBois. Jacob Hefner, forty-two, was working with his son when the roof fell in on them. The younger Hefner was able to escape with only minor injuries, but his father was fatally injured. The *DuBois Courier* reported that he died before he reached the mouth of the mine.

In August, "a Slav" named Steve Lesok was killed at the R&P mine in Adrian. Lesok was reportedly dropping cars down to the coke ovens and was standing on the end of one car when two others struck the rear of the car he was standing on. He was knocked down and the cars ran over him. He died a short time later.

Steam was often used in the mines for a variety of purposes. That led to a fatal accident on September 3, 1903. Albert Swanson of Elanora, a Swedish immigrant, was employed as an engineer in a new 278-foot shaft near Punxsutawney. He was being lowered in a bucket to the bottom of the shaft to work on the pumps. He was to have remained there for about fifteen minutes. When he failed to ring the electric bell to have himself raised, another worker became concerned and raised the bucket. When they looked into the bucket, they found that Swanson had been boiled alive by a broken steam hose. He left behind a widow and seven children.

The litany of mining accidents continued for decades before unions and the federal government stepped in to force improvements in mine safety and working conditions. As recent events in this county and elsewhere have proven, mining is still a very hazardous occupation.

## Baseball and the Boys in Blue

E.H. Clark kicked the dirt on the pitcher's mound, took a long look at the catcher, pulled back and threw the first pitch ever thrown in Brookville during an organized "base ball" game.

Clark and many others in Jefferson County were veterans of the Union army during the Civil War. They were the "boys in blue," and soon they became the baseball boys. Although there had been a few games of "town ball" played in Brookville, it took the army to give the game real structure. There is little doubt that the soldiers played baseball. Numerous letters mention playing the game, and a famous photograph shows the boys playing in the background while other troops drilled. It seemed that every time the army gave the troops some leisure time, someone would bring out a bat and a ball. After the surrender of the Confederacy in 1865, the troops were called to Washington, D.C. for a Grand Review. While waiting, they played baseball.

Following the end of the lumber rafting season, in June 1866, the *Brookville Herald* noted the formation of the first baseball team in town. They called themselves the Wild Cats. Many of the local men served in the 105$^{th}$ Pennsylvania Volunteers, which was nicknamed the Wild Cat Regiment. It seemed only natural to name the team after their old regiment. W.W. Corbett (a former colonel of the 105$^{th}$) was elected as the club's president. O.H. Brown was the vice-resident and J.P. George (who also happened to be the editor of the *Herald*) was elected as secretary. Both men were veterans.

Now that they were organized, the boys needed a place to play. The first ball field was "inside the new race course, below the Pickering Street Bridge," near where the Little League fields stand today in Brookville.

"Practice," said the *Herald*, "was to commence as soon as balls and bats can be procured." Those items had to be purchased from a Pittsburgh supplier. The early bats were bulbous things, and some models had raised rings around the base, showing the player where to place his hands. The balls were covered in horsehide and did not carry well. George Cook, operator of the Brookville and Kittanning stage line, donated the first ball to the Wild Cats.

A short time later, a second baseball team, the Excelsior Club, was organized in Brookville. They appointed a committee to procure bats and balls and to lay out the ground for the ball field.

On July 11, the teams were finally ready to play. It was an exhibition game between the first nine and second nine of the Wild Cats. The game was "closely contested and witnessed by a large number of spectators." There was no mention of a final score.

The game was new for the spectators, too. After seats were added to the ball field, spectators were asked to occupy those new seats, thus leaving the ground "free" for use of the players. A resolution was also adopted "inviting the ladies to witness the playing of the clubs on their days of practice."

Finally, on August 1, the two teams met for a "match game." The umpire was jurist W.P. Jenks and the scorer was Dr. D.A. Elliot. It was a close game, with the Wild Cat second nine defeating the first nine by a score of 46–37. The box score, the first to appear for any ballgame in the region, not only listed the hits for each player but also the number of outs the player recorded.

On August 15, the Wild Cats and the Excelsior teams played, with the Wild Cats winning 24–22. In that game, the Wild Cats had one home run and the Excelsior Club two. The Wild Cats made three "fly catches" and the Excelsior six. That is remarkable because the players did not use gloves; all of the catches were made bare handed.

Baseball was all the passion, and soon two clubs were organized in Punxsutawney: the Forest Base Ball Club and the Mahoning Baseball club.

The first game with an out-of-town opponent was held on August 28, when the "baseball fraternity" visited Clarion for a game against the Reserve Club of Franklin, which they lost 57–31. In the spirit of good sportsmanship, the players retired to the Alexander House for a "sumptuous" repast before heading home.

In late August, the first youth game was held for boys under sixteen. The Young America Club of Brookville defeated the Green Valley Club of Punxsutawney 99–36.

In September, cracks began to appear in the bond of good sportsmanship. The second nine of Brookville went to Punxsutawney, where they expected to play their opposites. Instead, they were met by Punxsy's first nine. The Brookville boys objected but played anyway, losing 58–20.

The early players also had their share of problems with umpires. In October, the Wild Cats went to Punxsutawney for a game and found one of the opposing players also acting as umpire. "It was evident from the commencement of the game that the umpire was determined to defeat the Wild Cats," stated the *Herald*. By the time the ninth inning rolled around, the Wild Cats had taken enough and walked off the field amid derision from the fans. The newspaper's coverage of the event may have been a bit biased as the editor was also one of the Wild Cats' outfielders.

The same editor commented that during a game with the Surprise Club of Brockway, the sun caused more balls to be dropped than normal by the outfielders. The editor (and outfielder) may have been the first to use the excuse "The sun was in my eyes."

In October, a "muffin" game was played by a group of "elderly gentlemen" including Sheriff Shannon and Esquire Marlin, who served as the team captains. "Each player was cheered as he took the bat," reported the *Herald*, "and the efforts of the fielders to avoid the ball sent to them was decidedly amusing." Shannon's team won the contest 59–48.

Baseball has changed over the years, but the game the boys in blue brought home has endured.

# Part II

# Inventors, Prophets and Scalawags

## The Scripture Rocks

A casual walk around Brookville can lead to an unusual discovery: stones carved with biblical verses. Long known as the "Scripture Rocks," they are the handiwork of one man, a man who was an enigma to his contemporaries and remains a puzzle today.

An educated man of obvious abilities, Douglas M. Stahlman gave up all his worldly possessions and dedicated himself to what he believed was his mission. His mission was to engrave biblical verse on 160 boulders. Between 1907 and 1911, Stahlman and two other men carved verse into the largest boulders they could find around Brookville. These were the Scripture Rocks, but they were only a portion of the 500 stones that Stahlman called the "Dedication Rocks."

Stahlman recorded his work in a series of journals that runs to two hundred pages. "There are over 500 rocks dedicated, every one stands for some Bible truth," he wrote. "For example there are rocks of faith, hope, love, obedience, salvation, holiness, peace and quietness."

Stahlman was born in the village of Kirkman in Jefferson County on August 17, 1861. He graduated from the Erie Commercial School and lived for fifteen years in Valparaiso, Indiana. In his journal, Stahlman speaks of his wife and children, although it is uncertain what became of the family.

Stahlman came back to Brookville in a roundabout fashion. He said he began his trip in New England with only a few cents and a Bible. He was able to make the trip by train through the generosity of his "brothers and sisters in faith."

In July 1906, Stahlman wrote that he was "divinely called to give up secular work." He said he was not conscious of what work he would do

Montgomery Stahlman's Chapel Rock.

or what form his service would take. He stayed at a local boardinghouse, where he compiled three religious leaflets and twelve cards. He gave these to 1,500 people.

Stahlman wrote in his journal that before the snow had melted he had become aware of a "place of prayer" in the woods north of the old Port Barnett School, where he had been "spiritually called." Prowling around the woods, he found a large rock with a flat stone beside it. Stahlman used the rock as his place of prayer. Stahlman began giving Bible readings at the rock until the first part of September.

From the dedication of that single rock, Stahlman's life's work took shape. The rock was located on an upper hillside and was about twenty feet high and forty feet long. The boulder had a projection that could shelter fifteen people. Stahlman wrote that he was conscious of a "marvelous spirit of prayer" and knelt on the roots of a hemlock tree that grew from the top of the stone. Stahlman dedicated this rock, naming it "Chapel Rock."

Stahlman began giving Bible readings at Chapel Rock, and the next week five men gathered to hear him. Stahlman said the "seal of divine approval" was given by the healing of one of the men of a "bodily affliction."

Soon after, Stahlman dedicated "Altar Rock," which stood nearby. Word of his preaching spread, and in early May 1909, seats were placed in front of Altar Rock, where seventy people could sit and listen. Soon

The Altar Rock showing seating for worshippers.

a roof was put over the rock. In quick succession, three more open-air chapels were erected.

Stahlman was not satisfied, however. He dedicated thirteen rocks from July 1908 to April 1911. "This ought to convince fair-minded people that this matter was not rushed into hastily, or without the greatest care," wrote Stahlman.

Stahlman said that it had been suggested to him that he carve the names of the rocks on them, but he admitted that he had no experience in that line. Undaunted, he set to work with a spike, scratching the names on the stone surfaces. The work stopped during the winter but resumed in the spring.

Stahlman began work every day at 5:00 a.m. and would work until 8:00 p.m. He had been provided with a mason's point and a mallet. With these tools, he began to carve large letters with double outlines.

"The work was entirely new to me but God helped and directed me and good progress was made from the start," he wrote. In his "rock book," Stahlman wrote that of the more than 160 carved rocks, "125 are in letters 12 inches high, a goodly number in letters 24 inches high and a few 30 inches high."

Stahlman remained unsatisfied. In the winter of 1911, he began spending all his days at Altar Rock. In March 1912, he removed himself from civilization and began the life of a hermit.

"I had not a cent of money and did not know where my next food or lodging could be obtained," wrote Stahlman. "My changeable clothes

This boulder is one of several that Stahlman carved between routes Pennsylvania 28 and U.S. 322 east of Brookville.

had been worn for a week without washing, the outer ones were decidedly shabby and the sole of one shoe was worn through so my big toe touched the ground in walking."

He slept at the outdoor chapel at McConnell's Mills. "My bed consisted of dry leaves spread on planks resting on the cross planks of the frame, about eight feet above the ground and my only covers for about 10 nights were heavy papers," he wrote. He later added a heavy horse blanket, "which had scarcely been used on a horse at all."

Stahlman spent seventy of the next seventy-seven nights in that bed of leaves "in more satisfaction and contentment than many a millionaire enjoys on his downy couch."

His fare was as sparse as his clothing. In twenty-three days he ate just twenty-two meals, which consisted of berries as they ripened and apples that were given to him. One day while he lay near a popular picnic area where some children were eating, he "prayed they would leave me some of their dinner on the ground, which they did."

During those weeks, Stahlman said he walked between 150 and 200 miles "over brick, concrete and dirt roads," dedicating rocks as he went.

A rock carved by Montgomery Stahlman.

The week after Christmas 1911, Stahlman enclosed a small room with rough planks on the southwest corner of Altar Rock under the roof formerly used for meetings. On March 14, 1912, this small ten- by twelve-foot room became Stahlman's home.

"Any spiritual person ought to realize at once something of the value of living in a place dedicated to God as this rock has been," he wrote.

The Port Barnett hermit had become a concern for the Brookville community, and in 1917 he was committed to the Dixmont Hospital in Pittsburgh. He spent the final twenty-five years of his life in the asylum, far from his beloved rocks.

During his confinement, Stahlman wrote, "If this dedication of rocks cannot withstand the same kind of attacks and criticism that the Bible has withstood through the centuries, it ought to fail and come to naught. It is presented as God's work and if God does not protect and make use of it, then let it go under."

Stahlman's Scripture Rocks remain. They have not gone under.

## Brookville's Birdman

The bustling, smoke-filled city of Pittsburgh came to a standstill on June 15, 1912. Pittsburghers were accustomed to noise. The steel city resounded with the awesome sound of the mills. The city streets were usually crowed with trolleys, vying for space with the wagons and automobiles. The Mon and the Allegheny teemed with the traffic of commerce—barges, tugs and passenger boats. Noise was nothing new to Pittsburgh. There was a new noise in the air on that Saturday morning. This sound came not from the rivers, roads or mills but rather from above.

Thousands of Pittsburghers stopped in their tracks and scanned the skies looking for something they had read about but few had ever seen: an airplane. A few lucky people caught a glimpse of a man soaring in the smoky sky in a very frail biplane. The man at the wheel of the Curtiss airplane was Earle Sandt, Brookville's "birdman."

Sandt's flight captured the heart of the steel city. His flight, the first ever over Pittsburgh, received a two-page spread in the *Pittsburgh Post*. The *Post* reporter wrote, "Risking his life to the treachery of a gale and battling with the elements, Earle Sandt thrilled the city by his spectacular flight. Fighting with superhuman efforts he conquered and won for himself the plaudits and gratitude of the metropolis."

Earle Sandt landing in Schenley Park, Pittsburgh, following his historic flight over the city. *Courtesy of David Taylor.*

The little airplane "raced at 100 m.p.h." and "soared with the grace of swooping eagles, clipping the edges of dangerous skyscrapers" and "rose to a height of 2,500 feet." Shrill sirens from steam whistles on river boats and from factories greeted Sandt on his flight.

Earle Sandt had written another chapter in early aviation history.

Sandt was a product of his times. Born in Brookville in May 1888 on the south side of town, Sandt grew to adulthood during the birth of the internal combustion engine. Suddenly released from the restrictions of steam, industrialists began to seek employment for the new invention. Ford and others were making automobiles, and the Wright brothers had finally solved the problem of heavier-than-air flight. Anything seemed possible.

While attending public school, Sandt displayed an aptitude for mechanics. He reportedly wired an entire building for electric lights. He became infatuated with the internal combustion engine. He owned the first motorcycle in Brookville and one of the first automobiles.

In 1909, at the age of twenty-one, he moved to Erie, Pennsylvania, and went into the automobile business with his brother. Sandt was not destined to remain on the ground for long, however. When word reached Erie of the Wright brother's flight at Kitty Hawk, Sandt began to look to the sky. To a person like Sandt, anything was possible. It was merely a matter of mechanics.

In 1911, Sandt attended the Curtiss School of Aviation in Hammondsport, New York. The instructor was none other than the legendary Glenn Curtiss himself. At the time, Curtiss rivaled the Wright brothers in notoriety and innovation. Curtiss was also a pioneer in the development of seaplanes.

Sandt had little problem with mastering flying. The next step was the purchase of an airplane from Curtiss. He made his first flight on Thanksgiving Day 1911. It was less than a success. Sandt was not injured, but his "machine" was destroyed. The early airplanes were made of plywood and canvas and had a tendency to have what would today be called massive airframe failures—they fell apart in midair. The small gasoline-powered engines were also known to quit. That was not quite as bad as an airframe failure since the "fliers" could often glide back to earth.

It was little wonder that the common man, saddled with a horse and buggy, thought the aeronauts were just plain nuts.

Undaunted by his first failure, Sandt bought his second machine and began practicing by flying off the Lake Erie ice in January 1912. By February 20, 1912, he felt confident enough to attempt a flight across the lake at its widest point. The destination was 32 miles away at Long Point, Canada. If successful, Sandt would become the first man not only to fly across the lake but possibly to make the first international flight in the western hemisphere.

Wrapped in a heavy fur coat, Sandt settled behind the wheel of the Curtiss and rose into the frigid air. Many watching his departure felt that they were bidding him farewell forever. Amazingly, Sandt had no problems on the flight to Long Point, and only thirty-two minutes after he left Erie, he touched down in Canada. The great lake had grown a little smaller.

Sandt was not so fortunate on his return trip. Opposite North East, a short distance from Erie, the engine quit, and Sandt was forced to make a landing on the ice. After a cold four-hour walk, Sandt reached shore. Search parties were unable to locate the wreckage of the Curtiss, however.

Not long after his feat at the lake, Sandt signed a contract with C.R. Cummings of Aero Exhibitions of Erie to perform his daring feats across western Pennsylvania. His good fortune in finding a sponsor did not improve his luck in the air.

On May 19, Sandt was giving an exhibition at Erie's Waldameer Park before two thousand people when his machine "volplaned" and dove into a knoll from a height of seventy-five feet. Sandt elected to hit the hill and avoided crashing into the crowd of spectators. He avoided serious injury by jumping out of the aircraft moments before it hit the ground.

Earle Sandt taking off from the frozen bay at Erie, Pennsylvania, on February 11, 1912. *Courtesy of David Taylor.*

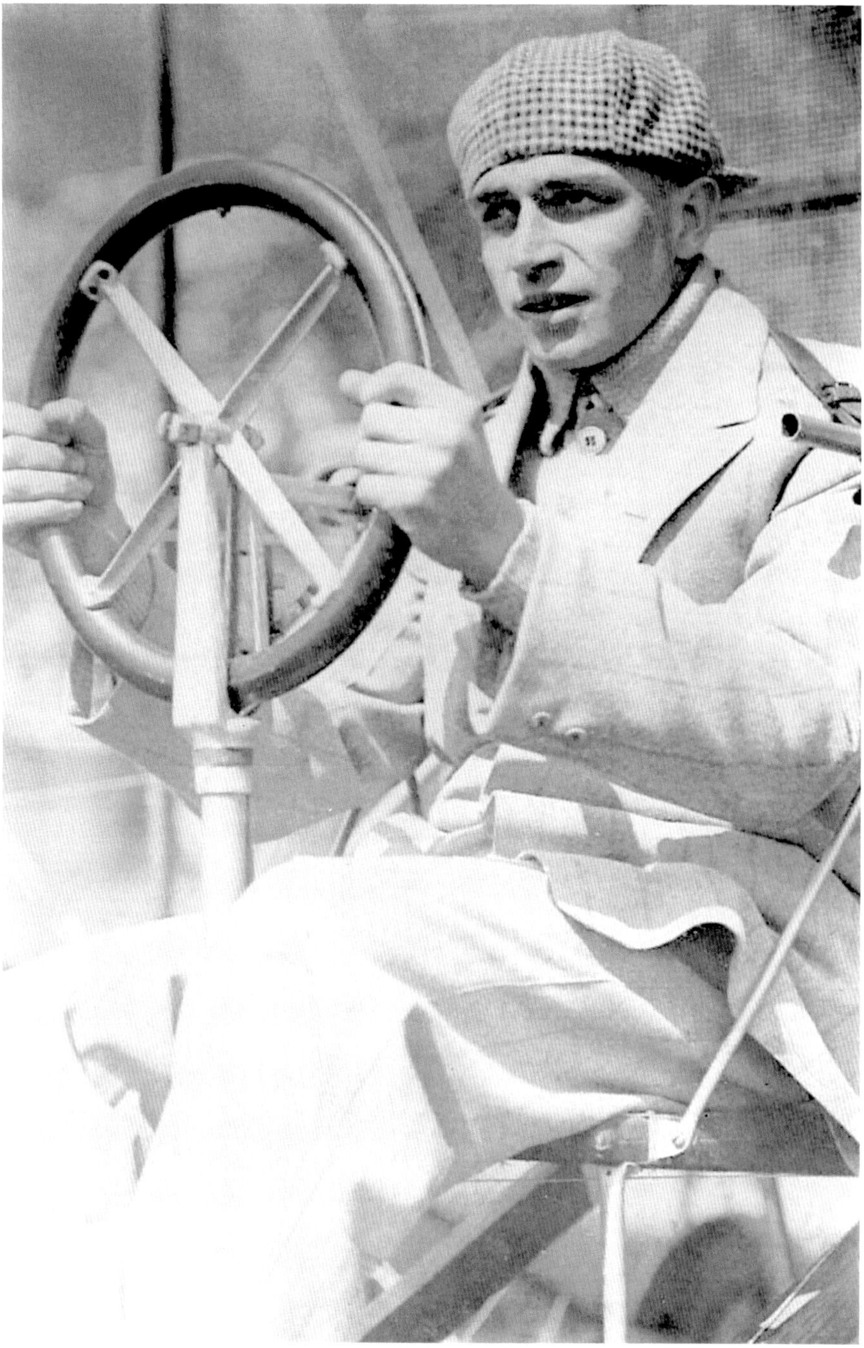

Earle Sandt in his Curtiss biplane, 1912. *Courtesy of David Taylor.*

Showing amazing resilience, Sandt purchased yet another airplane, and on May 30 set a new record. He flew to a height of 7,800 feet. On landing, Sandt said that he could have gone higher but that it was "too cold."

Following a pair of exhibition flights over DuBois, Sandt agreed to fly from Brookville to Punxsutawney. His sponsor, Mr. Cummings, visited both towns to secure the funding and, more importantly, the landing field.

Sandt planned to take off from the north side of Brookville, near the old high school. In June 1912, the Curtiss came to town packed in several crates. Sandt and his mechanic assembled the airplane. A large crowd assembled to watch Sandt and his cousin board the airplane for the attempt. They didn't get very far. Attempting to clear a house at the end of the street, a wing clipped the structure and the craft crashed. Neither Sandt nor his cousin suffered any injuries beyond a bruised ego. The plane was repaired by June 20, and this time Sandt made the flight alone.

Sandt continued to fly over the summer but not without mishap. During a show at Conneaut Lake, the biplane's engine quit, leaving Sandt powerless at two hundred feet. Sandt, becoming quite accustomed to these abrupt landings, once more threw himself from the airplane just before it crashed "to avoid contact with the engine." The Curtiss had the engine placed behind the pilot giving it the nickname of a "pusher." Sandt was knocked unconscious but suffered few other injuries.

During the winter of 1911–12, Sandt stayed in Brookville, working on the design of a "hydro-aero plane," which was successful. It was the last visit that he would have with his parents.

Sandt resumed his exhibition flying schedule in 1913. While flying over Grove City, Pennsylvania, Sandt's Curtiss was caught in a violent downdraft. The little flier was pushed into the ground, striking a building. Sandt was thrown clear of the wreckage but suffered a compound fracture to his arm and a broken leg. The injuries did not appear to be life-threatening, but tetanus set in and on June 26, 1913, Earle Sandt died of lockjaw. He was twenty-five years old.

Pioneers are remembered in many ways. Continents, cities, rivers and streets are named for them, or statues are erected in their honor. Others lie in great marble tombs, while some are nearly forgotten. Earle Sandt's pioneering effort is remembered on two plaques, one at the DuBois-Jefferson County Regional Airport and the second at the old Greater Pittsburgh International Airport. In 2009, the Commonwealth of Pennsylvania honored him when a state historical marker was erected at his birthplace in Brookville.

## Twyford's Folly

A curious crowd assembled on Main Street to see what R.E. Twyford had been boasting about. Twyford, a Pittsburgher, had convinced a number of local people to invest in his novel idea, an automobile. Twyford claimed that he could build an auto that was "the only machine in which power is applied to all four wheels." Twyford had invented the first four-wheel-drive vehicle, or so he claimed.

Twyford has secured a U.S. patent on his drive system, and that was probably a factor in selling stock in his company—a lot of stock. It must have been seen as a logical solution for the problem of poor country roads. If some of the other new autos could get around with power applied only to two wheels, imagine what a vehicle with four-wheel drive could do.

A large brick building was erected on the outskirts of Brookville, near the railroad tracks, in which Twyford could begin manufacturing his invention. A small sales brochure depicts the plant as a rectangular, two-story building, immaculately landscaped. Unfortunately, it is only an artist's drawing. As with most things associated with Twyford, the reality was different. Another page shows a picture of the interior of the plant with at least six different

Proving his point, R.E. Twyford pulls a series of buggies along Brookville's Main Street.

Twyford models on display. Further in the booklet are enlarged drawings of the "Tonneau" four-seater; the two-seat "Runabout"; a "Stanhope" with a collapsible top; an "Express" that had a truck bed with a curiously exposed engine; and a "Delivery" with an enclosed bed but an open engine.

It is believed the only car Twyford ever produced was a Runabout.

What drew people to Main Street in August 1905 was Twyford's claim that his vehicle could "climb all maximum grades or go through any ordinary depths of mud or snow or over unpaved streets and roads." Twyford humbly said in his sales material, "The advantage of double traction cannot be too highly estimated."

Now he was going to prove it. Twyford put his car to the test in a series of maneuvers worthy of P.T. Barnum. He made certain that everything was photographed and used in his sales booklet. The first photo shows Twyford at the tiller of his nine-horsepower Runabout. The rear wheels are raised six inches off the ground, and the car is being "hauled by the front wheels showing one advantage of the four-wheel drive."

A second photo has the Twyford climbing over a short stack of boards, which demonstrated "the ability of the Twyford to climb the curb or any other obstruction which is impossible for any other make." This was made

The Twyford Motor Car factory in Brookville shortly after it was closed.

Twyford demonstrates the power of his four-wheel-drive vehicle by elevating the rear wheels, using only the front wheels to propel the car.

possible by an "oscillating front axle, allowing one of the front wheels to rise 10 inches above the grade of the road and the other wheel to drop 10 inches below the grade of the road without twisting the body of the machine. This feature is found in no other make of machine."

Twyford must have enjoyed proving his critics to be wrong, and he wasn't even done yet. He had a wooden ramp built on Main Street at a twenty-five-degree angle, hitched two vehicles loaded with ten passengers to his tiny car and pulled them to the top of the ramp.

This was possible because "the power is equally applied between the rear and front axles and again equally distributed between the four wheels." Twyford said that this "compensation" prevented any drag between the "hind truck and the front truck in making a curve."

This application of power, said Twyford,

> *will not slip or skid on a curve and when on a slippery place or in the ditch will not slide along but will pull out which is saving of quite an annoyance and which does away with the lapping of rope on the wheels of rope on the*

> *wheels and also dispenses with other appliances on the tires or rims of the wheels which are expensive and also a source annoyance and which throws a great deal of mud and dust.*

In an era when autos looked more like buggies, mud control was an important feature.

To cap off the day's exhibit, Twyford hitched a series of eight buggies and wagons, carrying forty passengers, to his Runabout and, starting from a standstill, pulled them down the street in high gear.

Twyford had made his point. He boasted of a number of advantages including: double traction, power steering, transmission, rigid machinery, continuous compensation, application of power, three brakes, oscillating front axle, speed change, tractive force, compensation between front and rear and solid axles without steering knuckles.

He claimed that his auto was "the safest, simplest, most economical and most durable machine in the market" and perhaps it would have been. There was just one hitch: the car never made it to the market. The company sold stock several times but never was able to produce cars in any quantity. It has been alleged that Twyford's mechanical genius failed him when he attempted to replace the steering tiller with a steering wheel. Eventually, the money ran out and so did Twyford.

He left Brookville and the building that bore his name. His investors felt betrayed, and even the mention of his name was certain to draw critical comments. Nothing was heard of Twyford until 1916, when a local doughboy who was serving with General Pershing on the Mexican border wrote home stating that he had seen a truck using "the Twyford system of propulsion." It was a four-wheel-drive truck.

Brookville area resident Bill McCracken was intrigued by Twyford and sought any plans, drawings or photos of the single Twyford car. He painstakingly recreated a fully operational version of the Runabout and it worked. The repli-car is now on display at the Jefferson County Historical Society's museum in Brookville.

## THE WHITE ELEPHANT

It was intended to be a monument to community pride that would last for generations. Instead, it soon became a bad joke, useless, a "white elephant."

Since 1915, the White Elephant has stood on the Brookville Park grounds, a gleaming testament to an age when anything seemed possible.

Brookville in 1915 was sharing in the age of miracles. The Solar Electric Company lit the homes of the borough, plans were made to erect streetlights, automobiles putted around town, the Summerville Telephone Company brought people closer than ever before and a few brave souls were even taking to the air in flimsy flying machines. Anything seemed possible if people worked together.

Early in 1915, a drive was launched to raise money to build a YMCA in Brookville. Over $40,000 was raised for the project within a few months. Coupled with several church projects and a tremendous outpouring for evangelists, a total reaching nearly $150,000 had been provided for worthy causes.

The purchase of land for the Brookville Park was among the number of those good causes. Formerly the Brookville Fair Grounds, the thirteen-acre site along Sandy Lick Creek was bought in 1914 by the Brookville Park

The Park Auditorium under construction.

Association. The ambitious plans for the park included tennis courts, a racetrack and a ball field. The crowning glory to the new park was to be an auditorium.

The reasoning behind the project was a straight "business proposition." The editor of the *Brookville Republican* estimated that the county teacher's institute, an annual event, would bring about $15,000 to Brookville in a few days. The institute had been held in Reynoldsville for a number of years because the county seat had no hall large enough to hold the six hundred county teachers. Conventions, chautaquas, the fair and even reunions were all considered as possible customers for the new auditorium.

Initial plans called for a "fireproof" brick and tile building that could seat 2,500 people. The cost would be about $8,000. A three-man committee, consisting of W.N. Conrad, L.A. Leathers and Dr. J.A. Haven, canvassed the town to see if there was enough support to merit the effort.

Ample support was available, or so it seemed. In late April 1915, the group announced the launching of a new whirlwind campaign beginning on May 4. It would last one week and would, hopefully, raise the needed $8,000. Nine teams gathered at the church for their first meeting. The enthusiasm was high. The first meeting justified their expectations. Pledges of $1,993 were given at the "go-off."

The following night the teams reported another $1,600 in contributions. It soon became apparent, however, that the group needed to expand the drive to include pledges gathered on Friday. The group needed $980 even after the receipts for Friday were counted.

The dedicated group refused to admit defeat. Despite a rainy, cold night, the men decided to go out once more, determined to get the last few dollars they needed. They met again at 10:00 p.m. "Soaked to the skin," the one hundred volunteers held their collective breath while the pledges were counted.

Their efforts, late at night, had stirred the town, and a large crowd had gathered to hear the results. Practically a house-to-house effort had been made: "doorbells were rung, people aroused from their beds and men approached on the street," leading to many an "interesting encounter," according to the local newspaper accounts of the time.

When F.V. Deemer's team reported, the goal was not only reached, but surpassed. A total of $8,150 had been pledged within one week. The announcement caused hats to be thrown into the air and loud cheering and automobiles parked outside to "have their horns tooted."

The White Elephant during the Jefferson County Fair.

The committee lost no time in getting the project started. In June, the Pittsburgh firm of Kennedy and Company was engaged to design the building. The employment of the Pittsburgh company led many people to believe that the building was patterned after a Pittsburgh opera house, although that cannot now be determined.

At this point, the park board's optimism outgrew the original plan. Instead of the modest $8,000 building originally planned, a more expansive $25,000 auditorium would be built.

On August 16, 1915, ground was broken for the Park Auditorium. At the same time a board of seven "auditors" was appointed to oversee the work.

The construction, done with local labor, was slow. Even the formal dedication was several weeks late. Finally on September 30, 1915, the stone was laid. Cut into the surface was the simple inscription "Erected by the people, 1915." The stone was hollow, and copies of all the county newspapers, a list of county and borough officials and a list of the subscribers were place inside and the stone sealed, "to be opened by generations yet unborn."

A cattle show in the Park Auditorium.

Construction lagged even further behind. The steelwork was not in place by the end of 1915, months behind the scheduled completion date. It would not be until October 1916 that the roof was finished, a full year behind schedule. Local residents, faced with the unfinished structure every day, soon became skeptical, doubting if the "white elephant" would ever be finished. Even if it were completed, they asked, what could be done with it?

Rumors soon began to circulate that the money had been misappropriated. This prompted the park board members to publish a full list of expenditures. The ledger was printed in the *Brookville American* and totaled staggering $19,068.69, far more than the original subscribers had contributed. Clearly, the project had gotten out of hand. The money was gone and the building was far from finished.

A donation from W.N., J.M. and Lee Humphrey, owners of a brick manufacturing plant, contributed all of the brick needed to construct a sixty-one- by forty-foot stage. An appeal was made to launch another whirlwind campaign. The local newspapers lobbied the women of the town to conduct paper drives, give minstrel shows and other money-raising schemes.

A full railroad car of paper was collected, but the efforts fell far short of the needed capital. The park directors dug into their own pockets, but that also had a limit. The park directors eventually admitted defeat and signed the building over to a new organization, the Brookville Improvement Association for one dollar per year.

The new association was a stock company, but it can hardly be said that the goal of the group was to make money. Indeed, the reverse seems to have been true. To raise money for the completion of the building, four hundred shares of stock were sold at $50 per share. In return, the investors would be paid four percent per annum. This raised about $20,000.

By the end of the year, the building was under roof and the stage was completed, but the auditorium lacked a heating plant and seating.

World events overshadowed any attempt to finish the building. The United States entered World War I in 1917, and the homefront took a backseat to the war effort.

It wasn't until 1919 that local newspapers mentioned the first use of the White Elephant. The event was the Jefferson County Fair, the very function that the auditorium was built to support. That summer an auto show was held in the building.

The renovation project at the Jefferson County Courthouse began in 1927, forcing the county to seek other lodging for the various offices and the Court of Common Pleas. The only building in town large enough to house the county government was the White Elephant. Naturalization Court was the first legal proceeding held in the temporary quarters in June 1927.

As the weather turned colder, it became painfully clear that the auditorium needed heat. The Pittsburgh and Shawmut Railroad came to the rescue of the freezing politicians and donated a fifty horsepower boilers and fifty-foot stack.

The courthouse renovations were completed in 1928, and the politicians moved back up the hill, leaving the White Elephant empty once more.

*Jeffersonian Democrat* editor John F. McMurray wrote:

> *There is such a thing as setting a standard too high, or having a false standard. In the enthusiasm of starting a new project, a proper sense of proportion is often lacking. We have one notable example of over-enthusiastic and out of proportion ideas in Brookville, the Park Building, into which a good many thousands of dollars have been sunk and little, if any, real benefit has ever been derived. Let us keep our goals high but not so high that they will become a burden on the community.*

The White Elephant lived up to its name until the Sylvania Corporation moved into Brookville early in World War II. The White Elephant was incorporated into a complex that made tubes for radar units. After the war, Sylvania continued to operate the plant until the 1960s, when the shift to transistors left the tube-making Brookville plant a white elephant for Sylvania itself. The plant closed, leaving almost seven hundred people unemployed.

Once again, the White Elephant became a symbol of futility until the property was purchased by a small precision machine company. It has been a reminder to the community of the result of the collision between dreams and reality.

## BROKEN GLASS DREAMS

The free enterprise system allows people to succeed or fail, and failure is a hard teacher, as a group of turn-of-the-century Brookville capitalists learned.

In February 1902, the *Jeffersonian Democrat* "leaked" an item to its readers. The paper referred to something just ahead for Brookville that involved Brookville attorneys "Mssrs. Carmalt and Strong." The item stated that at the insistence of the two men "expert glass makers were making careful studies on the quality of the glass sand in the area which they reported to be in exhaustless quantity."

A short time later, everyone knew that Brookville would soon have its own glass factory. A new company was formed as a New Jersey Corporation and named the Brookville Glass and Tile Company.

Seven directors were named to head the fledgling endeavor; representing the stockholders were Judge Henry Truman, businessmen R.M. Matson and W.N. Humphrey, attorney N.L. Strong, P.J. Allgeier and August Boulnager. Florey Mauriocourt sat on the board as representative of the skilled workmen. Mauriocourt's seat on the board was intended to prevent any labor problems, but that idea, like many other innovations associated with the company, shattered like so many glass shards.

Almost immediately problems started cropping up. The lack of structural steel forced a delay in construction, and it was not until November 1901 that enough steel was secured for construction to begin. Enthusiasm was high when work began on the new plant in 1902. The estimated construction cost was $85,000.

The Brookville Glass Company factory.

The plant would produce a welcome shot in the community's economic arm. About one hundred men were to have worked at the plant when it reached full capacity. Very few local industries started with higher hopes.

The all-brick factory was originally to house an industry that was said to be at the forefront of industrial advances at that time. But the method for glassmaking was still dependent upon glass blowers. The system required additional construction. A tank building, flattening and tempering building, cutting house and box building were needed. An office was also required.

Insurance maps from the period show three separate buildings connected by passageways. Across the road stood yet another building, the batch room. All of these buildings were required by the process employed at the plant. At that time, the process began with a ball of molten glass that was gathered by lung power through a large blow pipe. The glass was blown into a cylinder, which was taken by a "snapper" who drew the glass into a one-fourth-inch-thick cord and wrapped it around a cylinder. The snapper then cracked the cylinder and flattened the glass in an oven. The glass was then sent through a tunnel, similar to a tempering oven, where it was cut into various sizes for shipping. A by-product was a curious glass cane that became very popular with the residents in the community.

The system was labor-intensive, requiring many skilled and unskilled workers. The wages were not good even in a period known for low wages. Payroll records indicate that the average wage during construction was ten cents per hour. The men worked six ten-hour days every week. Men like

Albert Ferraro and John Olson toiled in the quarry for ten to twelve dollars per week. Nor did the wages improve after the factory opened. The low wages and the growth of the labor movement in the nation were already posing a threat to the fragile glass industry.

There were other problems as well. In 1902, the company announced that it was temporarily ceasing its operation due to a lack of natural gas. The company stated that in the future glass would be made from gas derived from coal. In 1903, the factory advertised for stone "broken into boulders one man could handle." The advertisement specified "silica or sand" subject to inspection. The price was seventy-five cents per ton.

A national glass trust had been formed in 1903 and allegedly fixed the price on glass. The effect on small local plants was devastating. Several area factories cut wages by 12 percent. Orders were down and labor unrest rose.

In 1904, the Brookville Glass Company shut down. A meeting of glass manufacturers was held in Mount Jewett, resulting in an agreement to cut wages by 20 percent. It could not have been a surprise when the members of the Window Glass Workers union tendered their resignations. They gave seven days' notice, stating, "We will stand by organized labor to uphold wages but we will not stand the whips of slave drivers."

A nationwide meeting of glass producers was held in Cincinnati in April 1904, and prices were established for the industry. Elected as vice-president of that consortium was none other than N.L. Strong of the Brookville Glass Company. As 80 percent of the nation's glassmakers were present, the agreement was hailed as the end of the "plate glass wars."

The installation of new glassmaking equipment in 1915 was heralded as the salvation of the Brookville factory. Once more, the investors were to be disappointed. Legal battles erupted over the royalties to be paid on the new machines. The lawsuits would drag on for years.

In 1902, the company had a net income of $106,459.25, but the debts had also risen sharply. In October 1922, a U.S. Court of Appeals ruled on the royalty lawsuits, and although the plant had been idle for almost two years, plans were made to resume production once more.

It was believed that it would only take about two weeks to get the factory running again. The two weeks turned into months, and it was not until March 15, 1923, that Norman Stewart lit a match under the old tank. It would take another two weeks before the tank would be hot enough to make glass again.

The Brookville newspapers reported in April 1923 that the factory was running at near capacity and would employ two hundred men if they should be available. The enthusiasm was frustrated again, for the last time.

On August 18, 1924, the Brookville Title and Trust Company foreclosed on the plant and sold it at auction. F.C. Deemer bought the property for $10,000, which reportedly did not cover the cost of his investment. The corporation ceased to exist at that point. The old works were razed in 1963, but for years children walking along the railroad tracks near the site would discover chunks of green glass, the residue of broken dreams.

## Marlin's Amazing Opera House

Visitors to Brookville look baffled when they are told that the small town is home to a nine-hundred-seat opera house. They will look up and down Main Street, searching for some grand structure created in the European style. They will look in vain until they are told to look not right or left but up. There, sitting on the second and third floor of the Marlin Block, is the opera house, hidden in plain sight.

The builder of the hall, Colonel Silas J. Marlin, never intended for his pride and joy to be hidden. He believed it would be enjoyed by generations to come; it just didn't work out that way.

Silas Marlin was a man of many parts. He was a patriot, lumber baron, active citizen in the community and the father of the first Brookville Volunteer Fire Company, which he humbly named, "the Silas Marlin Hook and Ladder Company." He did purchase all of the equipment, which he believed gave him a certain advantage.

Marlin was a native of Indiana County. He settled in Brookville in 1852 and went into business as a merchant. At the outbreak of the Civil War, he joined first the 105$^{th}$ Pennsylvania Volunteers and later the 148$^{th}$ Pennsylvania Volunteers. He was appointed colonel by President Lincoln for his meritorious service at Ream's Station, Virginia, in 1864.

Returning to Brookville after the war, he went into the lumber trade, making a tidy fortune. Always active in civic affairs, he was named a director of the Brookville Water Company and joined the Grand Army of the Republic, an association of Union Army veterans.

His greatest legacy to the town was the sprawling structure that he built on Main Street. Made of "fire-proof" brick, the self-titled Marlin Block

The exterior of the Marlin Opera House.

was an ambitious endeavor. Marlin purchased the property in 1883 and razed the existing structure. He then went to work, and when the block was completed, it was the largest structure in the town, even eclipsing the Jefferson County Courthouse.

The street-level floors were occupied almost immediately, but the work on the opera house lagged. It was not completed until 1886. An early description of the opera house states that it is sixty-two feet wide and ninety feet long. The stage, which spanned the entire width, was eighteen feet deep. It was said that the stage could accommodate 120 performers. Two dressing rooms were added, one on either side of the stage.

When the opera house finally did open in 1886, visitors could count eight distinct sets of scenery, a drop curtain and a heavy curtain of dark cardinal velvet looped with golden cords. At the center of the curtain was a "beautiful picture in a gilded frame." The seating was divided into three levels: parquet, parquet circle and the family circle (or gallery). The hall was lit by 110 gas burners including a chandelier, footlights and house lights.

The main floor of the Marlin Opera House, looking north.

The interior of the Marlin Opera House, showing the balcony.

Marlin was a better builder than promoter. He failed to attract any professional entertainment for his grand opening and instead invited the citizen band to play. During the heyday of the opera house, the noted Confederate spy Belle Boyd appeared, as did the famed Jubilee Singers in 1894. Marlin did book a few operettas and minstrel shows, but the days of live entertainment were numbered. Edison had invented the motion picture, and the world of entertainment would never be the same.

After a twenty-year career, Marlin closed his opera house. Three years later, he died.

The seats have been removed and the curtain is gone, but the faded elegance of Marlin's opera house can still be seen, reflected in the chandelier suspended in time.

## THE BACKWARD THEATRE

The marquee is empty, the seats are torn and the stage is bare, but not long ago these old, abandoned buildings were alive with people enjoying the most modern entertainment available.

At one time every town, large or small, had at least one motion picture theatre. They were not located in shopping centers but rather in the heart of the community. Brookville's Columbia Theatre stood on Main Street, where it entertained and informed the people for decades. The Columbia was similar to other theatres built during the motion picture industry's early years, but it had one notable difference, a difference that made it an entry into Ripley's famed *Believe it or Not* series.

Motion pictures were not exactly new to Brookville residents by the time the Columbia opened its doors. As early as 1909, "picture plays" were being shown at the Fetzer Building. Although the content of these early shows was not recorded, the impact was. Mr. Zeller charged fifteen cents to view *The Perils of Pauline* and similar fare.

Frank Scribner operated a small theatre in the old Heber Building for about ten years from 1910 through 1920. He refined the event by adding the

The Columbia Theatre, showing the elevation in the rear that gave the movie house its unusual design.

One of the promotional stunts commonly used to promote new films was this stripped airplane parked at the Columbia Theatre. The movie was *Young Eagles* starring Buddy Rogers. The movie was billed as being "greater than *Wings*."

accompaniment of Gertrude Allgeier on the organ. Scribner was forced out of business when the Columbia opened.

The new theatre was spacious and offered its patrons a comfortable lobby and a restaurant. The lobby was on the ground floor of the New Jefferson House Hotel.

The local press was treated to a sneak preview by the owners. The editor of the *Brookville American* wrote:

> *The entry has a tile floor, marble decorations and built-in panels. Out in front is a marquee and above it a beautiful flash electric sign with the word "Columbia." Between the entrance and the foyer are swinging doors with panes of glass...The floor is linotile, from the ends flash mirrors, above is an arched ceiling and the walls are painted in pink, green and gold, the colors used in the main body of the theatre.*

Two entrances led from the lobby to the theatre. A sloping ramp was employed rather than stairs. It was about at this point that movie fans may have noticed something very different about this theatre. The ramp sloped upward away from the movie screen. The theatre had been built backward! Due to the topography of the town, the theatre could not be built in the usual fashion. To allow for five hundred people in the audience, the builders had to turn things around. For decades, customers entered the theatre only to find the audience looking at them!

One of the finer features of the old movie house was a pipe organ, a big improvement over the pianos usually used in smaller theatres. The stage was also equipped with scenery for use in live productions. A special curtain was used for motion pictures.

The owner of the theatre, the F.K. Brown Company, was lauded by the newspaper for its efforts in bringing such an "educative art" before the residents of the town.

The theatre was heated by steam, carpeted in the aisles and had "mellow" electric lighting. The lobby was furnished with white wicker furniture and a fountain in the center, complete with an illuminated castle and goldfish. Velvet wall hangings completed the picture of elegance.

The opening of the Columbia was well attended by the community. The stirring epic *Tarzan the Ape Man* was the first picture to be shown. At the organ was Professor A.P. Larson of Chicago, who remained in town for several days. In the future, the organist would be Ruby Buffington.

Following the first show, which ran just one day, Douglas Fairbanks starred in *He Comes up Smiling*. While the picture may not be memorable, the show was accompanied by a showing of the *Gazette News*, the first newsreel shown in Brookville.

On New Year's Day 1919, a patriotic film "with a cast of 40,000, shot on six big reels" depicted U.S. soldiers in action on the western front in World War I. The admission to this spectacular was twenty cents.

D.W. Griffith's *Hearts of the World* followed, accompanied by a ten-piece orchestra. Every show was detailed in a program. Clearly, going to the movies was an event.

The stage in the Columbia was not limited to motion pictures. Newspaper accounts tell of a wide range of events, including Mrs. F.C. Caroll's fashion show on "the corset you should not wear."

Benefit showings were often given, including the movie *Sadie Love* with Billie Burke for the Brookville High School. A benefit for employees of the Shawmut Railroad was offered with reduced admission of ten cents.

Vaudeville also played the Columbia. In November 1920, shows boasted "six pretty girls" and played for two days. The local newspapers, for once, did not critique the Columbia's performance.

The versatile nature of the theatre was evidenced when a theatre party was given for the Bandmaster of the USS *Connecticut* when he visited Brookville.

But it was the movies that kept the people coming back to the Columbia. All of the big stars of the silent era appeared on the backward screen—Chaplin, Swanson, Pickford, Arbuckle; all made their appearance. As the years wore on bank nights, talkies and color added to the movie experience. The aging theatre continued to be the center of entertainment until another medium altered America: television.

The Columbia was closed, reopened and closed again. Today, it has been restored and serves as a teen center, where Christian rock bands play in the backward theatre.

## MRS. MARLIN GOES TO VOTE

The elderly lady pulled her shawl closely around her neck, covering her against the early November chill. Slowly, with the aid of her son, she entered the Jefferson County Courthouse and climbed the stairs to the second floor.

Waiting for her there were a number of curious men, a photographer and some very proud women. Silently, they watched as Elizabeth Marlin, Brookville's oldest resident, entered the voting booth and local history.

In the general election of 1920, Mrs. Marlin became the first woman to vote. It was something that the community's women had been waiting to see for over half a century. The moment was captured by a local photographer, and the event became front-page news for the Brookville newspapers. The memorable event was the final scene in a long, long struggle.

The roots of the local suffrage movement can be traced back to May 1871. The final lecture of the season brought to Brookville one of the pioneers of the suffrage movement, Susan B. Anthony. Her address, "The Power of the Ballot," was "delivered to an appreciative audience" if not to a capacity crowd, according to local newspapers. The papers also observed that the speech "doubtless made some converts to her way of thinking or at

Here at 7:10 a.m. on November 2, 1920, Mrs. Elizabeth Marlin becomes the first woman to vote in Jefferson County. She voted in the Jefferson County Courthouse. Her son, B.M. Marlin, is on the extreme right in the bowler hat. Emerging from the voting booth is L.C. Scott. Fred D. Sayer is on the left. Squire William Truman and A.L. Endress are seated with their backs to the camera. Al Bauer and G.C. Endress are facing the camera.

least created a more friendly feeling toward the principle of women suffrage than had previously existed."

The *Brookville Republican* found the address to be "highly argumentative" but "less eloquent and the delivery below the standard expected of so distinguished a speaker." The newspaper did not summarize the address given at Nicholson Hall but felt that the heat may have kept the size of the crowd down and not the twenty-cent general admission charge.

The local suffrage movement resurfaced in June 1914, when Miss Mary E. Blakewell, "a prominent suffragist" from Pittsburgh spoke at the Jefferson County Courthouse. This time, there was no general admission. Her comments were not recorded, but in the same week local newspapers did report that the Progressive Party added a universal suffrage plank to the platform.

During this period, the adoption of legislation allowing women to vote was not considered a national issue but was left to the individual states to decide. By 1914, ten states had granted that right to women.

The issue was forcibly debated at Brookville's first chautaqua in the summer of 1914. Mrs. Bella V. LaFollette, the wife of a fiery Wisconsin senator, joined her husband on the tour. They met with the secretary of the Ohio Anti-Suffrage movement, Lucy Price. The debate was held, appropriately, on "Women's Day" and drew a large crowd.

The verbal jousting went unrecorded in the local press, but the *Republican* summed up the stance of Mrs. LaFollette. "Not a minor star, like the wives of so many celebrities, the orator felt the vote would enhance the woman's role in the home. Add rhetoric coming from a university graduate, author, lawyer and mother of four."

The pair was joined by a third advocate for reform, Mrs. Glendower Evans of Boston, who spoke of her interview in the White House.

The ball was rolling, and in 1915 Governor Brumbaugh encouraged the passage of a resolution altering the state's constitution to allow the vote. Both of the delegates from the Jefferson County area voted for the resolution, but it was defeated. The issue was placed on the general election ballot that year in the form of a referendum.

The other pressing social issue of the day, Prohibition, dominated the local newspaper columns and led one female reader to challenge the *Republican* to say something in favor of equal suffrage.

The challenge was picked up with a vengeance. In March, the paper came out with an editorial promoting the passage of the referendum. "This fall," said the newspaper, "husbands are going to vote whether they want their wives made their equals legally as they are now morally."

Three county newspapers all came out in favor of suffrage, causing the *Republican* to note, "The sentiment appears to be all the one way at the present time."

In July, the "Women's Liberty Bell" made a stop in Brookville, accompanied by three speakers. The bell literally weighed a ton and was eventually shipped to the Great San Francisco Fair. The bell was a replica of the Liberty Bell in Philadelphia with a few notable variations. The inscription on the bell read "establish justice," and the clapper was chained, a message that spoke louder than the tone of the bell ever could.

The bell was met by an honor guard of county women and escorted to Brookville. Pickering Street was closed when the bell was displayed. The local organizer of the event, Mrs. W.N. Conrad, and two of the women accompanying the bell, Louise Hill and Harriet Grimm, spoke to the enthusiastic crowd.

The *Republican* urged the women of the county to nominate a woman for the Brookville School Board, as a woman had already been elected to the school board in Punxsutawney. In September, Carrie B. Jenks, a graduate of Vassar, was elected with 472 votes. Ironically, she held the position for five years before she could vote for herself.

Jenks's election was small compensation when it was learned the suffrage referendum had been defeated in the general election. The local newspapers called the defeat the work of conservative "eastern voters" and predicted the "ultimate victory of a right cause." That ultimate victory had to wait for a larger victory in World War I.

The national movement had won important victories, and the Nineteenth Amendment was adopted by Congress pending approval by the individual states. This time, the measure was passed in Pennsylvania, and the stage was set for the historic vote in 1920.

That right did not come without a cost, however. The Jefferson County Commissioners published a notice stating that women who intended to vote would need to pay an occupational tax amounting to thirty-eight cents, the lowest classification for male voters.

The vast new pool of voters was not ignored by the major political parties. Women were seated as "advisors" by the Republican Party in August. For the first time, women were seated on a political committee. The Republicans named Mrs. Lex Mitchell, Miss McGee, Mrs. William Darr and Miss Ida Finnecy to the committee. The air was finally cleared in the traditional smoke-filled backrooms. The women became active almost immediately, staging rallies throughout the county.

The great moment came when Mrs. Marlin dropped her ballot into the box. Mrs. Darr was on hand to serve tea but was stopped by Bill Truman, the judge of election, who felt that this had to be a violation of the Eighteenth Amendment, although he wasn't sure how.

The times had indeed changed.

## PROHIBITION BECOMES PERSONAL

The battle lines were drawn in 1915. The forces for change were arrayed to carry their crusade to its conclusion, but opposed to them was a powerful and determined foe. The issue that split voters in Jefferson County did not fall across party lines but across a bar. The issue was Prohibition, but it did not go by that grand title.

A "No License League" had been formed with the announced goal of putting a man on the bench of the Court of Common Pleas who would carry out its program. Such a man was attorney Charles Corbet. His opponent was the incumbent judge John Reed, Corbet's brother-in-law. This election would be personal.

Under the Pennsylvania Brook's High License Law, each county could decide if it would be wet (with alcohol) or dry (without alcohol) by granting, or denying, any application for a liquor license. In a one-judge county, the man on the bench could evoke Prohibition simply by denying all license requests.

That was exactly what Judge Criswell had done in 1914 in another county. All applications for liquor licenses were denied, and that county went dry.

Jefferson County still busters, an arm of the Prohibition movement.

Prohibition supporters felt that such a course of action would also be effective in Jefferson County.

The result was one of the most bitter political campaigns ever seen in Jefferson County.

Judge John Reed was a twenty-year veteran of the bench. During that entire time he had seen only one of his decisions overturned by a higher court. He had an unblemished reputation and was held in high esteem by his peers. All of that was about to change.

Reed interpreted the law strictly. Licenses were refused when proof was offered showing that the applicant had not abided by the requirements of the law. He continued to grant licenses to hotels, taverns and inns. To the fervent prohibitionists this would not do.

The *Brookville Republican* made Prohibition the issue of the campaign. For a full year prior to the election, every issue of the newspaper carried at least one pro-Prohibition story. At first the paper's editorials called upon Judge Reed to heed the will of the people and modify his position by refusing to grant license applications presented at the February License Court.

Frustrated by Reed's strict adherence to the law, the newspaper called the judge a man "owned by the wets, body and soul." Reed attempted to respond to the charge in a long statement based on the law. The *Republican* said that his view was nothing but "honeyed phrases."

Several candidates entered the primary including William McCracken, Lex Mitchell, C.C. Bencoter, Raymond Brown, Stewart Whitehill, Corbett and Reed. Under the laws at that time, judges were elected on a nonpartisan ballot. No party affiliation was required. If one candidate received more than 51 percent of the vote in the primary, he would be unopposed in the general election in the fall. If not, all of the candidates would be placed on the ballot.

Fearing defeat, the dry forces moved to solidify support for one candidate, Corbet. A committee was established to interview each candidate except Judge Reed. Whitehill later claimed that the only way to get the endorsement of the No License League was to pay the committee $10,000. That allegation was the basis of a suit filed against Whitehill. (The suit was later dismissed by Judge Bouton.)

In May, the campaign reached new depths. A DuBois newspaper and a Brockway newspaper both supported Reed. The *Republican* downplayed the endorsements as "insignificant" and even accused the editor of the Brockway paper of having taken money to support Reed.

Judge John Reed.

Judge Charles Corbet.

Attacks on Reed became more frequent and more intense. Reed, who was over sixty years old, was accused of wanting to be reelected so he could become the first rural judge to receive the new $3,000 annual pension. It was a charge that the judge denied.

Constantly maligned in the *Republican*, Reed turned to the *Jeffersonian Democrat* to answer his critics. The *Republican* dismissed Reed's reasoned arguments by claiming that the paper was not behind the No License League but rather was just "a humble private in the ranks for good government who tries to keep his powder dry so that he can take a shot once in a while at the enemy of the church, the school and the home."

The "humble private" was using a machine gun–style approach on Corbet's opponents. Whitehill was accused of being "a stalking horse to divide the temperance vote." Other candidates withdrew from the race.

The *Republican* also attacked Reed's ethnic supporters. "It is a fact," said the newspaper, "that foreign voters, Italians, Slovaks, Hungarians, Poles, Slavs, Lithuanians, are being herded together and driven to vote for Reed." The paper appealed to "good Americans citizens" to reject a candidate who appealed to that "class of voter."

With the primary election less than a week away, the *Republican* blasted Reed in a special judgeship issue. All of the old charges were dredged up again: Reed attacks preachers; Reed attempted to buy votes by sending beer to a miner's picnic; and a list of the judge's alleged weaknesses were included.

The campaign worked. Corbet received 4,888 votes and Reed 3,921. Darr and Whitehill were far behind. No candidate had received the majority, setting up a showdown in the general election.

Reed continued to campaign in spite of his setback in the primary. At no time did he attack his brother-in-law, nor did Corbet directly attack Reed. Corbet never publicly stated he would turn the county dry, but his surrogates had no reserve about making that pledge.

The division over Prohibition also split the county's Republican Committee. In the end, the committee placed a full-page ad in the *Republican*, supporting Reed. The following week, the *Republican* refused to run the ad again, stating that "liquor money" was involved. Other papers in the county had no such objection to printing the ad.

In the general election, Corbet defeated Reed by 614 votes.

The dry forces had won, and they anxiously awaited Judge Corbet's first License Court in 1916. Also waiting anxiously for that first test were forty business owners, hotel owners, tavern keepers and brewers, whose economic future would be decided by the man they worked to defeat.

The Jefferson County Courthouse was filled to capacity as the applicants presented their petitions to Judge Corbet. Representing them was none other than former judge John Reed.

After one of the dry attorneys had made a motion asking all of the applicants be refused on a technicality, Reed pressed Judge Corbet to rule on the motion, but Corbet said he would take it under advisement. Reed proceeded to lecture Corbet until the new judge reminded his brother-in-law that he was no longer the judge. This comment brought applause from the audience and a rebuke from Corbet.

The legal wrangling went on, case by case, throughout a long day. In his summation, Reed reminded Judge Corbet that the Brooks law was a "license law and not a prohibition law." He was legally correct, but that did not matter in his reelection campaign or in court. Lex Mitchell summed up the dry position by stating, "The granting of licenses under the Brooks law is not entirely a legal question but also a moral question."

Judge Corbet addressed each application in turn and, after reciting the facts, denied them all. In a classic case of legislating from the bench, Jefferson County had gone dry. The morality of the majority had been imposed on the people of the county, but the crusaders found that legislating morality from the bench was far easier than altering human behavior. That would be a lesson the county, and the nation, would learn with national Prohibition.

Judge Reed retired and enjoyed life until his death in March 1926. Judge Corbet was a one-term judge, losing in the primary ten years later to William T. Darr. Corbet died in September 1927 while visiting California.

In the end, the resolution of the great booze debate rested not on prohibition but on moderation. It still does.

## Puckerty Joe, the Friendly Hermit

"Puckerty Joe" was a hermit. Why the spare European man chose to live apart was never known by the people in northern Jefferson County. They knew that he was odd, and he became a rural legend.

The Bicentennial Edition of the *Brookville American*, published on November 1, 1976, stated that Puckerty Joe's real name was Joe Susolik. He was born in Austria and immigrated to America in 1901. He settled in what is known

Puckerty Joe.

as "Puckerty Gap" on a plot of ground between the Pennsylvania Railroad and Red Bank Creek in 1926.

He was either a carpenter or a builder, no one is quite certain, but it seems that he actually constructed many buildings in the gap, and the site was known as the "Puckerty Settlement."

Eleanor Michael Shields told local writer Tom White that when she was a little girl her parents took her for a walk down the railroad tracks from Coder to the Puckerty Settlement, where she met the man about which she had heard so much.

She said it was generally believed that a broken heart and an avenging spirit were what brought Joe to America. The story was that the love of his life ran off with another man, and the pair headed for the States. Joe is said to have followed with murder in his heart and a large knife in his hand. By the time he made it to America, time and sea sickness could have had a mellowing effect, and he gave up looking for his sweetheart and settled down to work on the railroad.

Eleanor met Joe during the summer of 1950, when her parents decided to take her along to visit Puckerty Joe. When they reached the settlement, Joe greeted them warmly and took "us all around and showed us his buildings and gardens."

"He salvaged everything that floated down the creek and fell off the trains," Shields said in the interview that appeared in the *Jeffersonian Democrat*. "His buildings and fences were built from pieces of boards and tin cans flattened out and anything else he happened to have. Here and there were dishes of food for the cats and rats. Apparently they knew they were appreciated and learned to get along together."

The shack where he actually lived was dug about two feet down into the ground, and the walls were double thickness with grass in between, so it would have been warm in the winter. There was a large coal cook stove against one wall. Eleanor thought that the men who worked on the railroad had brought it on the train for him. She said that they always looked after him and supplied anything that he didn't find along the creek or railroad or could barter for in Brookville. Joe's home was full of trinkets, and on the wall behind the stove was a row of silver spoons.

According to Eleanor, nothing littered the road, creek banks or the railroad from his place to Brookville and probably on downstream to Summerville.

In May 1951, Puckerty Joe was killed when he was struck by a train while walking along the tracks not far from Coder. Railroad employees and other people who had befriended him took up a collection to pay for his funeral. He was buried at Brookville Cemetery.

Joe, who valued his privacy above all else, had that ultimate anonymity in death. There was not enough money available to erect a headstone for him, and he lay in an unmarked grave until a series of stories about him appeared in the *Jeffersonian Democrat* forty-five years later. Concerned local citizens launched a "Pennies of Puckerty" campaign that raised enough money to place a marker at the grave of Puckerty Joe.

## CHARLES BOWDISH, A LIFE IN MINIATURE

What began as a small hobby for a Brookville man grew and grew into a show that has delighted thousands of people in western Pennsylvania. Perhaps it was only destiny that Charlie Bowdish would entertain people. His family operated traveling shows for decades and entertained locally. But it was Charlie who outdid them.

Bowdish performed in a few family productions, but it wasn't until after his service in World War I that his real talent became evident. Suffering from a heart ailment, Bowdish was discharged from the army. Unable to work in the real world, Bowdish created his own. It was here in his scale model world that Charlie Bowdish found his true calling.

Every Christmas, in his Creek Street home, Bowdish would assemble his village and create a display. He added Lionel trains imitating the rail lines

Charlie Bowdish at the Buhl Science Center.

that ran through Brookville. On Christmas Eve 1920, Charlie hosted his brother's wedding and reception and entertained the guests by running his train display. One of the guests, Alfred Truman, asked if he could bring some friends over to see the show. Word quickly spread, and nearly six hundred people showed up.

Bowdish soon began setting up and exhibiting his railroad every year during the Christmas season. Each year there would be a different theme. One year it was white Christmas and another year Indian summer. The display spanned the entire second floor, but no matter how large it became, Bowdish never charged admission. Thousands of people saw it over the years, often standing in line for hours. A flood nearly destroyed his stored models, and his insurance company questioned the safety of the crowds entering the old wooden house. Bowdish knew he had to do something if his small world was to survive. He entered into talks with local business leaders about erecting a new Bowdish display in a building he designed. The town leaders balked at the expense, forcing Bowdish to look elsewhere.

That "elsewhere" turned out to be the Buhl Planetarium in Pittsburgh. Bowdish moved the display to the Buhl Science Center in 1954, where it remained until 1990. The exhibit was an instant hit and remained one of the major holiday attractions in Pittsburgh. The display was in the basement, and the line would at times extend out the front door and around the block. The wait could be up to four hours long.

Pittsburghers lining up to see the Miniature Village and Railroad exhibition.

Bowdish would work almost around the clock to prepare the display for the season. Buhl renamed that area Bowdish Hall in his honor.

In 1992, the Miniature Railroad and Village was moved to the new Carnegie Science Center in Pittsburgh. The display still showcases at least 75 percent of Charlie's original creations at any given time. The 2,300-square-foot miniature exhibit recreates historic replicas of western Pennsylvania and includes several of Charlie's early American and Victorian favorites from the Brookville area.

Charlie Bowdish died in 1988, but his miniature world keeps on turning.

## A Novelty No More

No one in Jefferson County took them seriously. With strange names and delicate machinery, the automobile was looked at as a passing fancy of the wealthy. Automobiles just did not appear to serve any practical purpose. Nobody in his right mind was going to trade his horse for one.

Within a decade, however, public opinion changed, and the automobile was accepted as an indispensible part of daily life. That acceptance did not come easily or painlessly. Americans accustomed to matching the pace of their day to the gait of a horse now found that they could go zipping along at three times that speed. This new sense of speed and time altered the social fabric of the nation. No longer were small towns isolated and insulated. Now they were connected to communities that previously had been hours or even days away.

Automobiles arrived in the area in 1903. One of the earliest autos, a Thomas, was registered to Walter Sandt. That car was not the first gasoline-powered vehicle owned by Sandt however. The May 7, 1903 *Jeffersonian Democrat* noted a trip taken by Sandt to DuBois on his motorcycle. Sandt made the twenty-four-mile trip in one hour and five minutes, "a little bit faster than we would care to ride on a machine of that kind," said John McMurray, the editor of the newspaper.

Soon a variety of autos were seen on Brookville's streets. Among them were a Locomobile, Maxwell, White Steamer, Pierce Arrow, Saxon and American. There were also others more familiar to modern drivers: Fords, Cadillacs and Buicks. By April, 1910, 30 cars were registered in Brookville and 11,400 in the state. There were also 7,100 licensed chauffeurs.

With the introduction of more cars came more problems. The first meeting between a car and a horse-drawn buggy is legendary. Part of the problem

Main Street, Brookville, lined with early automobiles.

was lack of decent roads suitable for autos. Many streets in Brookville were paved, but township roads were seldom improved. The slightest rain turned them into bottomless quagmires.

Learning to drive was no easy task either. Ford dealer L.A. Lathers opened his business before he learned to drive. He was seen on Main Street "taking his first lessons in learning to operate the 'machine.'" The machine was a 1910, twenty-horsepower, five-passenger touring car that Leathers offered for sale at the astounding price of $950.

Before long motorists were zipping along at unchecked speeds. The legislature sensed the potential for trouble and in 1909 set the speed limit at twenty-four miles per hour and twelve miles per hour in towns. It was the same speed set for horses. The Brookville newspaper noted that police officers in Kittanning had purchased stopwatches to aid in the apprehension of speeders.

County law officers were not slow in joining in the war on speeding. A paved section of highway between Reynoldsville and DuBois was known as "the raceway." Winslow Township constables set up the first speed trap along that road and reportedly "pinched" a score of drivers, some of them going as fast as thirty miles per hour.

While speeding was one problem, dust was another. The path of a speeding automobile on a country road could be followed by the plume of dust it raised. That problem would not be resolved until the state began a massive highway-building effort two decades later.

The old North Fork Bridge showing the condition of roads during poor weather. The roads made travel by automobile an adventure.

Travel by automobile in those days was a test of endurance and mechanical skill. Frequent breakdowns turned minor expeditions into epics. In 1907, John F. Brown took a drive from Clarion to DuBois, a distance of sixty-two miles, in just four hours, an unheard-of pace, and even more remarkably, the trip was without mishap.

N.D. Matson was not so fortunate. While driving near the village of Howe, just north of Brookville, the pin holding the steering mechanism together suddenly dropped out, falling on the road. The car "on its own fancy" climbed an embankment and threatened to tip over. The alert Matson and his companion jumped from the car and caught it, returning it to the road. The pin was retrieved and replaced, allowing the party to return home unscathed.

As the number of cars increased, so did the number of accidents. In one of the earliest automobile accidents in the area, the local newspapers reported that John Geist drove over a curb in Brookville, breaking one front wheel and stoving in a rear wheel. In the same issue, a reader stated the inability of the auto to climb a telephone pole. F.L. Verstine had an accident that is familiar today: skidding into a guardrail.

The first reported serious accident with an auto took place on Brookville's Main Street. In June 1911, Earl Stahlman, a workman at the Methodist church, decided to go home for lunch. Hopping on his bicycle, Stahlman

Main Street, circa 1930. The street had been paved, cars were everywhere and traffic signals were in the middle of the road.

went down Pickering Street but cut his turn a bit short, never expecting a car to be sitting in his path. He cut the running board of Verstine's car and his own head. He recovered and so did the car.

The first local fatality reported involving an auto occurred on Jefferson Street when a small boy ran into the path of car operated by Reed Brown. The boy was killed in what was deemed to be "an unavoidable accident."

America's new love was the car, and soon local motorists were pushing their machines to test their limits. Thomas Litch took his new Ford on a "record run" to DuBois, leaving Saturday and returning Sunday. He claimed the mud was "up to the axles," but he wanted to prove his car could go anywhere that a horse and buggy could go. It was generally felt that most horses had more sense than Litch and would not venture out in such weather.

D.L. Taylor had a set of electric lights installed on his Pierce Arrow so he could drive after dark. The work was done by the Automobile Specialty Company, one of several new companies that were springing up to serve the motoring public. The firm was located in the former Twyford factory in south Brookville.

A lively trade in automobiles soon began, giving birth to that American icon, the car dealer. Leathers had the Ford dealership, but he faced competition from H.R. Steele, who brought an Overland Run About to town and gave a demonstration. He then invited folks down to his dealership in Punxsutawney.

As early as 1904, the local newspaper said that "the bicycle created quite a craze for a while but never was much use. The automobile promises to fill a real usefulness."

A glimpse of that usefulness could be seen when J.A. McDonald bought a Ford to help him with his business. In 1911, Bill Henshaw purchased an International Auto-truck to carry passengers from the train station. The International carried nine people comfortably. This may have been the first minivan.

By 1919, the state had granted over 160,000 licenses (at ten dollars each), marking a new high point in the automobile's popularity. The editor of the Brookville newspapers noted that in one hour on a Sunday afternoon he counted nineteen automobiles going by his Main Street post.

The availability of cars inevitably led to the modern version of the horse thief. In 1916, Ed Frampton had the dubious distinction of being the area's first car theft victim. Frampton had parked his Ford near the Baptist church on a Sunday evening only to find the car missing when he returned. The next day, the car turned up a few blocks away undamaged. Frampton, a good sport, said that he hoped the boys who took it had a good time but that he wished they would have replaced the gasoline they had used.

The growing number of cars inevitably spelled the end of the horse's long reign. In 1901, the newspaper carried an advertisement for an auction at which a number of buggies were to be sold, the "owners having no use for them."

Cars were arriving with such frequency that the newspaper's practice of noting each new arrival was abandoned. By May 1910, there were at least fifty cars in Brookville.

The increasing absence of horses made many of the old-timers long for the old days. Editor John McMurray, a veteran of the Civil War, must have had that feeling in June 1913 when he saw a fine team of bay horses pulling a buggy along Main Street. "I would rather own that team with a $200 buggy than the most expensive automobile in this country," he said.

On that day, McMurray may have sensed that a way of life that he and the country had known was passing, and nothing would ever be as simple again.

## HEROES ALL

Andrew Carnegie once said, "Heroic action is impulsive." That truth earned Charles Hetrick of Brookville the Carnegie Hero Medal in 2007.

Hetrick's award was the result of an incident on the night of Thursday, February 23, 2006. That night, Hetrick rushed into a burning mobile home to rescue Martha Rich, a paraplegic confined to a wheelchair. Hetrick entered the burning trailer and crawled his way through the trailer looking for Rich. He found her laying face down on the floor, where she had slid out of her wheelchair. He rolled her over onto her back and pulled her along the floor about three feet at a time. Hetrick said that once he got Rich to the door, someone helped drag her onto the porch. Rich was briefly hospitalized. Hetrick suffered slight smoke inhalation.

Hetrick is not the first person from Jefferson County to receive the prestigious award. The award was just four years old when the first Jefferson County residents were honored.

A mine cave-in at Brockwayville on December 12, 1908, led to the recognition of four men. Miners Francis P. De Santis, twenty-eight; Guiseppe Petruccelli, eighteen; and Vincenzo Stefanelli, twenty, were attempting to rescue Michele Rubino, twenty-eight, who was caught by a fall of rock. They immediately made an effort to lift the rock but were unable to when another fall occurred, catching De Santis's trouser leg and pinning him to the floor and killing Petruccelli and Stefanelli. William P. Harris, thirty, the mine boss, helped to rescue De Santis. While other falls impended, Harris crawled close enough to hand De Santis a knife, with which he freed himself. Rubino, when released, was found to be dead.

Edward W. Noll, twenty-five, a brewery worker, died assisting in an attempt to save Patrick F. Williamson, twenty-two, brewery worker, from suffocation in Punxsutawney on January 10, 1910. Williamson entered a tank to save a man who had been overcome by fumes of amyl nitrite. Noll lifted the man to others at the top of the tank but fell unconscious himself. Noll collapsed while on the rim of the tank helping to rescue Williamson and was dead when taken down. Williamson was found to have died from the fumes.

James O. London, twenty-six, an assistant general foreman, died attempting to save Harry R. Hicks, eleven, from drowning in the Mahoning Creek. On June 30, 1912, Hicks, who could not swim, and an older companion were in deep water in Mahoning Creek, and they became involved in a struggle. London was on a dam sixteen feet from them and immediately jumped into the water, fully dressed, and swam to them. He caught hold of Harry, who struggled wildly, but before he could save him, all went beneath the surface. Harry's companion was saved by a man who extended a pole to him, but Harry and London drowned.

Michael Albanito, a forty-nine-year-old invalid saved seven-year-old J. Earl Woodford from drowning when he fell into flooded Elk Run in Punxsutawney. Albanito, who suffered from a serious heart ailment, ran 150 feet to the bank, jumped 8 feet into the water and groped with his hands for Earl, who drifted against him. Albanito carried him up a steep bank, where a man relieved him of Earl. Albanito suffered a heart attack as the result of his act and was confined to bed for forty days.

Frank D. Collyer, thirty-five, a locomotive engineer, saved Elizabeth Pifer, thirteen; Beulah, twenty-eight; and Robert E. Arthurs, nine, from drowning in Brookville on July 25, 1919. Elizabeth pushed a raft containing Robert into deep water in North Fork Creek, and the raft was then carried him beyond her reach. She started to swim toward it but became frightened and turned toward the bank. She lost control and sank. Mrs. Arthurs waded from the bank, and Robert jumped from the raft toward her and sank. Mrs. Arthurs then stepped into water over her head. She reached Robert under the surface and held him tightly to her and struggled. Collyer waded from the opposite bank and swam one hundred feet to Elizabeth, grasped her at the shoulder and swam with her to the bank. He then swam thirty feet and dived to Mrs. Arthurs, who was standing under the surface. Collyer took hold of her arm and rose to the surface with her. She put her left arm around Collyer, pressing his right arm to his side, and they sank together. Collyer was unable to free himself, and they rose and sank again. Collyer then broke the hold of Mrs. Arthurs and grasped her by the hair. Collyer swam with Mrs. Arthurs and Robert to the bank.

Bertha Markell Ohl saved Dorothy J. Smith from drowning in the Red Bank Creek in Summerville on July 30, 1932. While wading in the creek, seventeen-year-old Smith slid from a rock into water eight feet deep. She was momentarily submerged and was carried farther from the bank. Mrs. Ohl, twenty, who was a poor swimmer, swam to her. Smith grabbed her ankle. Mrs. Ohl jerked free. After a struggle in which both bobbed up and down, Mrs. Ohl broke her hold. Smith grabbed Mrs. Ohl's bathing suit, and she towed Smith until she grasped a pole that was extended to her. Mrs. Ohl was aided out of the water and was temporarily exhausted.

Alan R. Rowland rescued Isaac R. Smail from burning in a Punxsutawney building on December 30, 1974. When fire broke out at night on the second floor, Smail, ninety-four, left his third-floor apartment and tried to escape. Rowland, a nineteen-year-old college student, climbed to a balcony at the second-floor level and entered the building, where conditions were worsening rapidly. Flames were spreading onto the stairway, but Rowland climbed to the third floor. Although smoke limited visibility, Rowland located Smail and carried him down the burning stairs. Rowland took Smail to the balcony, where they waited until firemen arrived. Smail was hospitalized for burns but recovered.

The medal commission was established on April 15, 1904, and since that time more than nine thousand medals have been awarded in the United States and Canada. The Carnegie medal is a bronze medallion three inches in diameter with Andrew Carnegie's image on one side and a verse from the New Testament (John 15:13) on the reverse. It reads: "Greater love hath no man than this, that a man lay down his life for his friends."

## Flying the Mail

The lumbering Curtiss Jenny biplane was in trouble. Strong headwinds had nearly sucked the gas tank dry on the army plane. Major Reed Henderson desperately needed a place to set the fragile canvas-covered plane down. The countryside in northwestern Pennsylvania looked uninviting to the World War I ace and his engineer, Lieutenant Perry Powers.

Rolling hills covered with trees was no place to land the Jenny. Peering over the side, Henderson spotted an open area about ten miles ahead. Just over the hill from a small town was what appeared to be a racetrack, the perfect place to land.

The major swung the plane low over the town, attracting startled looks from the residents, lifted the plane just enough to clear the hills and landed in the infield at the racetrack. Moments later, people from the town raced out in their buggies, and even some 150 automobiles braved the road. It was only then that Henderson learned that he had landed in Brookville on the farm of E.B. Henderson. The date was August 8, 1919. The major obtained ten gallons of gasoline and continued on his way to New Jersey.

Henderson may have soon forgotten his emergency landing, but the people of Brookville did not. The airplane was the first to land in the area since Earl Sandt's flight several years before. A safe landing field was rare when the government decided to move the mail by air in 1919. Using surplus aircraft and army flyers, the U.S. Postal Service started airmail in 1919. It was a hazardous duty.

In the first two years, a dozen pilots were killed, often lost landing in emergency situations. The fact that a "safe" field existed near Brookville became known among the fliers. In late October 1919, two planes went down in the area while trying to locate the Henderson farm in bad weather.

Near Emerickville, a postal service biplane tried an emergency landing on the L.M. Shugarts farm, but the wheels became mired and the plane flipped onto its top wing in the wet soil. The pilot, Jack Knight, was uninjured. Knight became a national hero in 1921 as a member of a relay team of fliers who took the mail across the nation in record time. Brookville residents remembered Knight on one of his less famous flights.

At about the same time that Knight was coming to a hard stop, another post office plane, the notoriously underpowered DeHavilland and DH 4, was turning turtle in the soft earth of the S.C. Beeman farm near Corsica. Like Knight, the pilot was uninjured. Unflappable, the pilot calmly gathered up the mail, hopped a ride to Clarion and continued his route.

The planes were left lying in the mud for several days before new crews were dispatched to repair them. Both craft were more seriously damaged than was first thought, so they were flown to the Henderson farm, where they were dismantled for shipment. While the crews were engaged in their work, the *Brookville American* asked the fliers if they thought the farm could be used as an airfield. The response delighted the newspaperman. He learned that the field was considered to be "the best in this end of the state." The pilots felt that the field at Bellefonte was too small and the one at Clarion was rough and had drainage problems. The forty-acre site midway on the New York–Chicago airmail route was perfect for an emergency field.

Local citizens approached local congressman N.L. Strong about the venture, but the government moved slowly, even in those days.

By the mid-1920s, the sound of aircraft was almost commonplace in the skies above Brookville. One aviator was reportedly so familiar with the town that he flew low over the borough to salute the residents or, as the *American* reported, "possibly one certain resident."

During August 1920, another pair of biplanes were forced down at the Henderson farm. The mail from yet another downed plane near Reynoldsville was to have been picked up at the farm, but the anticipated plane never arrived and the first airmail from Brookville left on a train.

The post office constantly expanded its airmail routes, and the need to fly around the clock was apparent. Without modern electronics to guide the aircraft, a system of beacons was set up. One was to be in Brookville. By modern standards the idea was simple. Groupings of automobile headlights would provide about 1,500 candle power, rotating on poles from thirty to fifty feet high. The pilot could follow the lights on almost any night, and when a flight left New York the approach was phoned ahead and the lights were turned on. A total of 150 beacons were erected on the route. Emergency fields were also set up, thirty-two in all, and one was to be at the Henderson farm.

Finally, in 1925, the Henderson farm was officially recognized as an emergency field, six years after the beleaguered Jenny touched down. The airport is now a grassy field, but for thirty years it served area residents and the nation's fledgling aviation industry.

## Punxsutawney Phil

Jefferson County's most famous resident lives in a hole, is reclusive and has been known to snap at people. Yet, every February 2, thousands of people flock to his abode in Gobbler's Knob to listen to the unintelligible utterings of the "prognosticator of prognosticators," the world-famous "Punxsutawney Phil."

The legend of Punxsutawney Phil draws the world's attention to the small hill just outside Punxsutawney. People from around the world travel to see if the groundhog will see his shadow. It is common to find people from as far away as New Zealand, Europe and Asia who come to pay homage to the woodchuck. Attendance alternates between ten thousand and twenty thousand people. The mayor of Punxsutawney is busy with marriage ceremonies throughout the day, and people with birthdays on Groundhog Day feel the primeval urge to celebrate their big day with Phil.

The Groundhog Day tradition probably began in Germany. The Germans believed that if a hibernating animal cast a shadow on February 2, the Christian holiday of Candlemas, winter would last another six weeks. If no shadow was seen, legend said that spring would come early.

Since 1887, Phil has seen his shadow 100 times in 112 years. Records from the National Climactic Data Center in Asheville, North Carolina, show that his accuracy rate since 1980 is about 59 percent.

Phil is protected by the fifteen members of the Groundhog Club's Inner Circle, who plan annual Groundhog Day festivities. The Inner Circle members are also taught the language of the Groundhog, "Groundhogese." One of the Inner Circle members is charged with translating Phil's prediction, which would otherwise be impossible for mere mortals to decipher.

Punxsutawney Phil at Gobbler's Knob on February 2, 2009.

Each Inner Circle member has a specific duty, and not just anyone may handle the "seer of seers." The handler is usually the one wearing the heavy gloves.

In 2004, the Commonwealth of Pennsylvania recognized the importance of Phil by erecting a state historical marker at Gobbler's Knob. At the dedication, William Cooper, then president of the Punxsutawney Groundhog Club, said, "Our job and function in the Groundhog Club is to protect and to perpetuate the legend of Punxsutawney Phil. As we say, there are a lot of serious and important things in life, and Groundhog Day is not one of them."

That theme was evidenced in the 1993 movie suitably titled *Groundhog Day*, starring Bill Murray. The comedy made Phil a star and, like any star, Phil used a double for many of the scenes.

In recent years, other animal soothsayers have competed for the attention of the world on February 2, but the predictions of Staten Island Chuck, Georgia's General Beauregard and Buckeye Chuck just do not possess the magic of Punxsutawney Phil.

Phil also makes public appearances throughout the year. When he is not on tour, Phil and his companion, Phyllis, can be found in a heated hutch at the Punxsutawney Library.

# Part III

# From the Corridors of the Courthouse

## The Twice-Hung Man

Jefferson County residents were outraged when neighbors discovered the body of seventy-year-old widow Betty McDonald in her home near Brockwayville in February 1867. Suspicion soon fell on two men, Charles Chase and Dean Graves. The pursuit of justice followed one to Michigan and the other to the gallows, twice.

Charles Winton Graves was arrested in Brockwayville for horse theft and murder. He was taken to Brookville to face the murder charge. Graves made good his escape, prompting the county commissioners to offer a five-hundred-dollar reward for his capture.

The Charles Chase trial opened before a packed courtroom in May 1867. He was defended by the Jenks law firm. The commonwealth's case was prosecuted by District Attorney Lewis Grunder, assisted by John McMurray and I.G. and A.L. Gordon. Judge Campbell sat on the bench.

The complete transcript of the trial was printed in the *Brookville Republican*, attesting to the enormous local interest in the trial. Testimony lasted several days before the case went to the jury. The jury found Chase guilty as charged. Judge Campbell sentenced Chase to hang and for the sentence to be carried out on April 23, 1867.

A scaffold was erected between the courthouse and the old jail, the first (but not the last) to occupy that space. A fence was erected to enclose the area and to keep out idle spectators. On the appointed day, fifty citizens were sent to the rooftops of the adjoining buildings to keep away the curious. Only a few people were permitted inside the enclosure. One was a reporter for the *Republican*.

The old Jefferson County Courthouse with the jail next door. Hangings took place in the area between the two buildings.

The unnamed reporter said that Chase faced his end with courage. Chase maintained his innocence to the end. Confronted with the eight-foot-square, sixteen-foot-high scaffold, Chase remained "cheerful" but "paled" when he saw it.

The twenty-six-year-old Chase was dressed in black, matching the hangman's hood. When he reached the platform, he shook hands with the sheriff, the deputy sheriff and his attorney and announced that he would "die an innocent man." He asked God to have mercy on his soul.

Chase assumed his place, the hood was lowered over his head and the new rope adjusted. All was ready for Jefferson County's first execution. The trap was sprung and Chase fell—all the way to the ground. The rope had been improperly measured, allowing Chase to hit the ground. Chase said, "It's hard." The sheriff gathered him up, and at 2:18 p.m. the execution was performed again, this time with the desired effect.

In October, a telegram arrived in Brookville from Grand Rapids, Michigan, announcing the capture of Graves (and inquiring about the reward).

Graves, a "notorious character," was tried in December. He was also charged with murder and found guilty. He was not to be hanged, however. He was sentenced by Judge Campbell to eleven years and eight months in solitary confinement at hard labor in the Western Penitentiary.

The *Republican* concluded, "One has passed, guilty or innocent, into another world and his accomplice in crime retires, as it were, to an almost living death."

The murder of Betty McDonald was not the first in Jefferson County, however. That event occurred on April 24, 1844, when a long-standing dispute erupted in violence. James Green and Daniel Long were at odds over the ownership of a prime section of land in Jefferson County. The law supported Long, but Green and his son, Edwin, took matters into their own hands.

The Greens went to Long's remote cabin in what was then northern Jefferson County to settle the score. The Greens found the cabin empty and went in to lie in wait for Long. Soon the unsuspecting Long and a friend, Samuel Knopsnyder, entered the cabin, where Long was confronted with his own rifle, held by the elder Green. Without hesitation Green fired, killing Long. Knopsnyder attempted to flee but was overtaken and pummeled to the ground.

Daniel Long was the first man to be murdered in Jefferson County and Knopsnyder, who lingered for a few days, the second.

The Greens were captured and taken to Brookville, the new county seat, for trial. The indictment of the Greens accused the pair of "not having the fear of God before their eyes and being seduced and moved by the devil."

The case was controversial and so was the verdict. The pair was convicted, but much to the surprise of Long's friends, the sentence was only for four years of solitary confinement at hard labor at the Western Penitentiary. It was widely held that Green's friends had influenced the sentence.

As the population of the county grew, so did the number of murders. In July 1874, a farmer named Sanford Perry was fatally stabbed by Amil Sibley. The *Jeffersonian Democrat* stated that a "too intimate relationship with the wife of Perry by Sibley brought on the fight."

It appeared that Sibley had a solid case for self-defense as he had been attacked by a hoe-wielding Perry, but the case never went to trial. At last report, Sibley was "still at large."

In 1885, Curtis Terwilliger, a mild twenty-five-year-old graduate of Oberlin College, was charged with the murder of his stepfather, George Washington Dunkle. Newspaper reports of the time paint a poor picture of Dunkle. A veteran of the Civil War, Dunkle was said to have been a violent man who beat his wife and had a habit of throwing large stones at Terwilliger's head. The plea of self-defense did not fly with the jury, and Terwilliger was found guilty.

Scrawled on the original court docket is a recommendation for mercy from the jury. The twelve-man panel got its wish, and Terwilliger served just one year in prison and paid ten dollars in court costs.

The wave of immigrants brought many strange-sounding names into the court records. In 1885, three Swedes, all named Swanson, were tried for murder and sentenced to serve six years in prison and pay $1,000 fines.

The murder of Dan Reeves near Walston in 1891 brought three Hungarians to trial. John Horat, Steve Legera and Joseph Ur were convicted and spent the next eleven years in prison. The case marked the first time that an interpreter was required because the defendants could not speak English.

A Jewish peddler named Louis Helman met his end at the hands of William and Frank Dodson in 1896 near Brockwayville. The pair ambushed Helman and shot him several times. It was reported that Hellman put up a terrific fight, allowing his companion to escape and preventing the Dobsons from taking his money.

The pair were captured in Elk County and returned to Brookville for trial. They were convicted of voluntary manslaughter and sentenced to twelve years in prison in "separate and solitary confinement."

The rash of murders continued in the 1890s, culminating with the stabbing death of Louis Scalzi by his friend and neighbor, Joseph Aiello, on Christmas Day 1896.

In spite of a spirited defense by his attorney, Clay Campbell, District Attorney N.L. Strong won a verdict of guilty. The sentence was death by hanging. Campbell launched a thirteen-point appeal but to no avail. Aiello was the last man to be executed in Jefferson County.

The Commonwealth of Pennsylvania assumed the role of executioner early in the twentieth century, and capital punishment was conducted in state prisons. The old gallows site in Brookville is now a placid park, set aside to honor veterans.

## The Day Time Stood Still

The calendars may have read Wednesday, May 21, 1941, but for everyone in Brookville that day, it was simply known as "the day time stood still."

Unlike the rest of Pennsylvania, Jefferson County had not joined the march to daylight savings time. The county's timepiece, high in the courthouse clock tower, was off by an hour. This situation was not the result of any mechanical malfunction but rather the inability of the county commissioners to act on adopting daylight savings time.

Commissioners Homer Reitz, Gil Schuckers and Milt Sutter were not alone in their confusion over DST.

In late April 1941, the Brookville Borough Council postponed action on "fast time" in spite of a petition signed by four hundred residents favoring the change in time. Council stated there was a rumor that President Franklin D.

The Jefferson County Courthouse clock tower.

Roosevelt was going to proclaim Daylight Savings Time nationwide. Local attorney Thomas Stauffer presented the petitions, stating they represented about 80 percent of the town's merchants.

C.E. Smith, manager of the Columbia Theatre in Brookville, was opposed to the idea, stating that the issue should be put to a vote by the people. He said that he could see no advantage to the move unless the neighboring towns also adopted it.

Although the town council took no action, two of Brookville's largest employers, the Pittsburgh and Shawmut Railroad and Humphrey Brick and Tile, announced that they would adopt Daylight Savings Time effective the following Monday. The reason was simple: to save on power and light.

Bowing to public pressure, the council adopted Daylight Savings Time for the first time, effective May 10 at 2:00 a.m. Burgess Harold Thompson issued a proclamation stating that the measure was adopted to "avoid confusion" and because the state had adopted DST earlier, making it the official time of the state, "which may not be changed by action of any official or municipal council."

That change in the state law did not seem to register with the county commissioners.

"Little boys fighting over a clock is a familiar scene to hundreds," said Bill Carlton, editor of the *Brookville American*. "But when the boys happen to be county commissioners and should be spending their time on things more to the advantage of the taxpayers, it begins to get humorous. "Little Miltie Sutter, about six-years-old, Little Homer Reitz, chasing seven and Chubby Guy Schuckers, the same, had been bawling and close to running home to mama for three days, all because Miltie wanted the clock to register standard time. Homer wanted it to show daylight savings time and Little Guy just didn't give a damn."

The situation was brought to boil when "someone who should be kissed" went up to the courthouse clock and moved the big hands ahead one hour, making daylight savings time official. Except that the commissioners had not approved the time change.

According to the *American*, when Sutter came to work on Monday he proceeded to "rave, roar and rant." The paper stated that no effort was spared to find the time thief. "Janitors were questioned, the office forces were suspicioned, blood pressures soared and those in the know, laughed, and laughed and laughed."

This guerilla action led Commissioner Reitz to make a motion to solicit the opinion of the Court of Common Pleas. Until that opinion could be obtained, Reitz and Sutter voted to stop the clock at 11:05 a.m., Monday, leading to Brookville "standing time."

The three commissioners went upstairs to the court only to find that that body was already operating on Daylight Savings Time. Pressed for an opinion, the court reportedly replied that it had "no jurisdiction over the sun, the moon, or the town clock."

Left to their own devices, the trio of commissioners attempted to hammer out a compromise. Their first effort was to simply move ahead and adopt DST. That did not sit well with Sutter, who attempted to alter the motion by adding language that stipulated the statute of 1923 making Eastern Standard Time the official time in the commonwealth and that the new motion was contrary to that law. Reitz agreed to amend his motion, but Schuckers "suddenly developed an inability to speak" according to the *American*. The motion died for the lack of a second.

Time waits for no man, even county commissioners, and the following day Schuckers and Reitz formed an alliance and sent county maintenance man Milo Eisenhart up to change the clock. Sutter, according to the *American*, found out what was afoot and tried to stop time by trying to talk Reitz into changing his mind.

All the while, Eisenhart was slowly putting time back on track. The *American* said by the time Sutter was done talking to Reitz, the deed had been done.

"At exactly 2:30 p.m., the 'town clock' atop the Court House here tolled the hour of 12 and then a few minutes later tolled the hours of one o'clock and then two o'clock and finally the hands stopped at 2:30 and the clock was running on Daylight Savings Time," said the *American*.

Outside of the courthouse, "Brookvilleites who were on the street below in rather great numbers, stood in their tracks and every time Milo turned the hands ahead a few minutes, they cheered and cheered," said the *American*. And so ended the "battle of the town clock."

## Walls Did Not This a Prison Make

The town was wrapped in a deep sleep except for one industrious inmate at the old Jefferson County Jail. All of Saturday night he was busy working loose a bar on his second-floor cell window. Just before dawn, the bar came out, affording him a narrow avenue to freedom.

The Jefferson County Courthouse and the old county jail. The jail was not a secure place.

The inmate, Johnson by name, examined the gap and decided that it was too small to allow both his clothing and himself to squeeze through. He removed his clothes, dropping out of the hole. He wriggled his head and shoulders through the space but found he had miscalculated. He couldn't get his hips through. Worse, he found that he couldn't withdraw his head and shoulders. He was stuck.

Johnson braced the October chill until daybreak and then gave it up, calling for help from some of the boarders at the American Hotel just across the alley. Johnson was guided down to street level in what the Brookville newspapers said was "a scene not remarkable for its elegance."

Johnson's aborted escape ended in failure, but that was not the case for most freedom-minded inmates at the jail in the 1870s. In that single decade, with the jail not more than thirty years old, no fewer than twenty-six inmates made escapes. A dozen or more attempts were frustrated.

The decision to erect a new county lockup, replacing the original jail, was made in the 1850s. The imposing two-story brick and stone building was finished in 1856. Built at a cost of $14,200, the structure also contained the residence of the county sheriff. The jail stood on the southwest corner of the public square on Main Street in Brookville, next to the American Hotel.

County historian Kate Scott states that the jail was not quite a year old when the first escape attempt was made. She noted that the jail was "never a safe receptacle for prisoners" and was "entirely inadequate" by 1886. She was right.

In March 1869, the local newspapers noted the escape of "two jailbirds" who removed the lock on their cell, prompting the newspaper editor to remark that "the locks of this institution are entirely inadequate" and the pair of prisoners "escaped by the usual means of egress"—the front door. There was no mention in the newspaper of what the jailors or the sheriff were doing at the time of the escape.

A year later, two more inmates escaped. The newspaper commented that the "accommodations, not being to their entire satisfaction," caused the restive youths to depart. The local editor remarked that the jail was not so much a lockup but a "walk-out."

In May 1874, two more industrious inmates dismantled a chimney, crawled through the hole and, using a rope made of their bed clothes, scaled down the wall to freedom. Most of the escapes were made over the weekend, presumably at a time when the jailors' vigilance was relaxed.

Barely four months later, two men removed a large stone from the wall facing the alley between the jail and the hotel and made their escape. The local newspaper stated, "They have not been seen or heard of and no effort was made for their recapture."

Just one month after that escape, two more inmates escaped, doing what the newspaper termed "a la Barnum," and again "so little interest is shown that no person seems to know anything about it."

In February, a man had been captured after his first jailbreak and made a second successful departure from the jail. Again he displaced a stone and scaled the wall to freedom.

Not two days later, five men attempted to duplicate his escape, but they had not planned as well. They chose the wrong stone and pushed out a block leading to the interior hallway of the jail. They could go no further and were still roaming the halls when the sheriff caught them.

The newspaper called the jail a "mere farce," adding that "only those who truly love the place stay there."

A man named Pounds took a different turn in his escape in April 1878. He secured a key. He used an iron bar to loosen the cell bars. Where the iron bar came from was never fully explained.

Later that same year, Miss Hoover, who was acting in the absence of the sheriff, allowed two men to visit friends in the jail. When the friends departed, so did the prisoners, who made a rush for the door. Five made their getaway, and more would have made it out if two of the prisoners had not aided Miss Hoover in locking the door. It is doubtful that Miss Hoover was ever trusted with the keys again.

In September 1879, the sheriff granted special privileges to a man named Gillespie, who had confessed his crime. His faith was misplaced. Given the run of the jail, he helped three of his friends, and himself, run out of the jail.

"Every wide-awake rogue escapes," bemoaned the local newspaper, and so they did.

The old jail continued to be used until the remodeling of the Jefferson County Courthouse in 1927. When the work was done, prisoners were housed in a cellblock in the basement of the building. The new cellblock was "modern" by the standards of the day and remained in service until the county built the new jail almost six decades later.

While there may be an occasional escape from the new jail, it is highly doubtful that the county will ever witness another series of escapes similar to the rash at the old jail.

## A PLACE OF REFUGE

Most everyone in Jefferson County was familiar with the old County Home. For most of the twentieth century, the sprawling red brick structure at the end of the brick paved road stood in Pine Creek Township as a testament to caring.

The County Home was much more than a poorhouse, however. Early admittance records retained by Jefferson County show the County Home cared for not only the poor but also elderly, mentally infirm, ill and even orphans.

The first "inmates" were not admitted until August 1901. That first group included eleven men and six women. This marked the county's first attempt at caring for the poor. Prior to that time, the individual municipalities were responsible for that care. J.N. Kelly, the first superintendent of the new home, managed a building measuring 120 feet wide with an engine and laundry 42 feet wide in the rear.

The old Jefferson County Home was a refuge for the troubled and the poor.

The building was divided into "100 rooms or apartments" consisting of sleeping rooms, dining rooms, sitting rooms, chapel, bathrooms, toilet rooms and store rooms. The sanitary arrangements were also praised, especially for those in the "insane department." The building was divided by gender, and no "intermingling of the sexes" was permitted. The new home had the capacity of taking care of 150 inmates, but "by crowding up the apartments 250 can be accommodated" according to the *Brookville Republican*.

The early part of the century found Jefferson County with no modern hospitals and a lot of labor problems. One of the early admissions combined both of these conditions. In 1906, Vincent Carboni was admitted to the County Home. Described as a thirty-six-year-old white male, the miner was described as a "Member of Black Hand. He was shot at Florence by the State Police in a riot."

Not every story revealed in the records is quite so dramatic, but each sheds some light on the social conditions during that time. Robert Serrle emigrated from England in 1881 and went to work in the mines. In England, he had been struck in the head by an adz and suffered from dizziness. He entered the County Home in 1909 and stayed for two years. His doctor warned him against using whiskey or alcoholic stimulants. He was released to the care of his family.

William Buel, thirty-five, was a widower whose wife died in 1906. The barber was admitted in 1912 suffering from "chronic alcoholism." The diagnosis read, "For five years never was sober or knew what he was doing."

Perhaps the most distressing case histories involve children. Seven-year-old Vernon Lloyd was ordered to stay at the County Home in 1909 when his parents served time in jail. He was returned to them when they were released. There were many children admitted to the County Home.

In 1911, the four Tokorick children of Crenshaw—ten-year-old Gusty, nine-year-old Joe, three-year-old "Johny" and two-year-old Andy—were admitted. The boys were released and returned to the County Home every fall for the next three years. Eight-year-old Nadie Labonne was left at the County Home in May 1913 when his "father ran away with another man's wife. Mother would not take care of him." His father took him in five months later.

Frank Nega was twelve-years-old when he came to Punxsutawney with a man that became intoxicated and was locked up. The boy wandered about Punxsutawney for about two weeks when one of the county commissioners brought him to the County Home. He was later adopted by a local family.

Not every child was so fortunate. Harry White was three years old when he was sent to the County Home. His mother was serving time, first in the county jail and later in the workhouse. He died from accidental poisoning when he was given strychnine pills. He was buried in the Butler Cemetery.

His death was not the only accident at the County Home. In 1918, Frank Secrist, who was listed as insane, died from choking on a piece of beef. And not all of the deaths were accidents. In 1927, Sylvester Motheral went to the woods, cut his throat and died in the Brookville Hospital.

John Milliron was seventy-seven years old when he arrived at the County Home in a basket. He had fallen from a trestle and was badly hurt. He died two weeks later after being admitted.

In June 1917, James Reed was admitted, suffering from severe burns caused by the busting of a carbide lamp. He survived another eighteen days.

Curtis Boyle was forty-six when he was admitted to the County Home with "melancholia." He was described as "being feeble-minded since birth" but became worse since the death of his mother. He died at the home in 1915.

John O'Brian was described as a fifty-eight-year-old veteran of the English army. The "umbrella fixer" had been shot through the lungs while he was in the army and suffered from lung trouble. Homeless, he committed himself in December 1916 and died one month later. He was buried in Butler Cemetery.

Enoch Bergman was placed in the County Home when he was arrested as a vagrant. He simply "went away" in 1915. He was not the only homeless person to find refuge in the County Home. Minnie Glass arrived in February 1917 with frozen, gangrenous, feet. Described as a "working girl," she was sent to the Clarion County Poor Farm the next month.

The County Home also became a refuge for unwed mothers. In 1916, Barbara Eck was one of the many who arrived at the County Home and within a month gave birth to a child. The baby was adopted by a Brookville couple. Barbara returned to live with her parents.

The county commissioners were often responsible for admitting people to the County Home and, in at least one case, for discharging an inmate. In 1916, Maude DeLacy, a fifteen-year-old English immigrant, was sent to the home. Described as a "way-ward girl," she had spent nine months in the county jail. The commissioners initially gave the girl money to leave but later had to pick her up from the Reynoldsville lockup. Undaunted by the first attempt to rid themselves of the problem child, the commissioners then took her directly to the Clearfield County Home personally.

Another man, Vito Laurito, was sent on an even longer trip by the commissioners. Suffering from heart trouble, the forty-six-year-old miner was admitted to the County Home in June 1917. He was deported by the commissioners and sailed back to Italy in July 1919. He had $100 in his pocket, half furnished by the county.

Some of the inmates left of their own account. In 1921, A.W. George checked himself out because his "grub did not please him." He returned three more times before the County Home finally dropped him from the admittance records. George Briggs, a laborer, entered the County Home in 1921 and simply "left." His personal history states that he "left in 1921, don't know where…went down the brick road." And eventually, all of them—the sick, lame, mentally ill, orphaned—all went down the brick road and into oblivion.

## The Butter Battle

They were as guilty as sin and everyone in Jefferson County knew it. The county commissioners didn't even contest the facts, so it was no surprise when Judge John Reed found the trio guilty as charged in October 1908.

To some people the crime was more heinous than decent folks could imagine. Commissioners Al Hawk, Newton Webster and Harvey D. Haugh had toyed with nature and come down on the side of science.

Politicians back then, as now, had the reputation of being slippery, but these three were guilty of the most slippery of crimes: they had fed oleomargarine to the inmates of the Jefferson County Poor House.

The great Jefferson County oleo scandal began eighteen years earlier when oleomargarine was invented. Back in 1908, oleomargarine was not the staple of the American diet that it is today. It was seen by some as a blow to dairy farmers and by others as product of science that would pollute the body.

Clearly such an offense must be addressed by state statue and it was. In 1885, the state legislature passed an act that made it illegal to manufacture or sell oleomargarine. The offense was a misdemeanor punishable by fine or imprisonment or both.

The state refined that law in 1893, making it a misdemeanor offense to purchase or use oleomargarine with the intent of using it in charitable and penal institutions in the state.

But the use of margarine grew and was often purchased by the counties for use in poorhouses and jails. In Lycoming County, the board of commissioners had been caught spreading the margarine around, but they had quietly paid the fine and avoided further prosecution.

When the "pure food" officials descended on Jefferson County in early 1903, they found that the county was indeed violating the law and serving oleo to the guests of the county. In June, the state filed charges against the three commissioners and J.N. Kelly, the superintendent of the County Home.

The commissioners never denied that they had broken the law. Through their attorneys, they argued that the law itself was flawed—not to say absurd.

The *Brookville Republican* wondered why the county officials should be prosecuted when anyone could buy oleomargarine for use at their "sweet pleasure" any time they wanted.

The newspaper believed that the state expected the county commissioners to roll over and pay the fine. Hawk, Haugh and Webster were determined to have their day in court, however.

This would be the first time that the state had to prosecute a case under the act. State officials tried to smooth things with the commissioners in an effort to avoid going to court, but the commissioners put on a hard crust and insisted on their rights.

"They will no doubt suffer a sufficient penalty," said the *Republican*, "but such penalty will be determined in a court of law and not by those who earn the price of their place and position in the pure food department by unearthing some great wrong."

The oleomargarine case went before Judge Reed in September, and the state, "through its hired detectives," obtained a conviction. The state may have won the case, but Judge Reed knew which side his bread was buttered on.

In his ruling, he said, "I am convinced that the ends of justice will be fully met upon the payment by them of the costs, and in the aggregate the payment of a fine of one hundred dollars," concluded Judge Reed.

Kelly, "a good public servant," was not fined but had to pay the costs of the prosecution.

In the end, the great oleomargarine caper had proven the power of the state to make and enforce unpalatable laws and the wisdom of the people in toasting those who write those laws.

## The Reluctant Treasurer

Three new Jefferson County commissioners faced an almost insurmountable task: the county was nearly broke, the bills were due and there was just no money available to pay them. Before the county could get back on its financial feet, three commissioners were turned out of office and the county treasurer was jailed.

The date was January 4, 1932, and the commissioners W.S. "Billy" Reid, M.C. "Milt" Sutter and T.C. "Clint" McQuown were looking at a balance sheet that was way out of balance. It was the Great Depression and the impact of the initiatives launched by Franklin D. Roosevelt was still unknown.

The situation was bleak. The new commissioners had to pay bills that they had not incurred. The day after they took office, the new commissioners approved the payment of a note to the Jefferson County National Bank in the amount of $10,000. The note had been taken out by the previous board of commissioners only a month earlier. The money had been used to pay the county's bills.

The commissioners set the 1932 tax rate for the county at four mills (forty cents) on the $100; the county road bond at three mills (thirty cents) on $100; the courthouse bond at two mills (twenty cents) on the $100; and the poor tax at three mills (thirty cents) per $100. The courthouse debt millage and the poor tax proved to be very important in the years to come.

The dire financial situation that the county faced was underscored on January 26 when the county's salary board met to set the pay rates for the county's employees. Only one county employee, Julia Coulter, received a raise. That was $5, making her salary $70 per month. The salary board froze the salaries of those workers making less than $100 a month. They were the lucky ones. County employees who made more than $100 a month suffered a 15 percent reduction in pay. The only exceptions were the two janitors who had to work twelve hours each day so they could get the same money they received in 1931.

The salary freeze was not enough to pay the county's bills, however. In April, the commissioners approved a loan of $45,000 from the Jefferson County National Bank in Brookville to "meet current expenses" and to pay "certain outstanding obligations," which included election expenses. The loan would be repaid with six percent interest. The commissioners may have believed that they were getting ahead of the money problem when another dark cloud darkened their door.

In May, it was learned the Jefferson County Poor Fund had more bills than it could pay. In those days, the county maintained its own "poor farm," the County Home in Pine Creek Township. Over $24,000 in overdrafts from the poor fund were paid from the county's general fund. That was still not enough and the county was forced to borrow another $5,000 from the Jefferson County National Bank.

Money was getting so tight that traditional donations by the county became bones of contention. In June 1932, when the Brookville Fair Association made a request for an appropriation of $100, Commissioner Sutter voted against the motion. He said, "I believe at this time a fair is a detriment to the county as so many people will attend the fair when they need their money at home for food and clothing." The motion carried two to one.

Sutter was right; things were not good in Jefferson County. There were so many properties scheduled for sheriff's sale that the commissioners petitioned the court to postpone the sale for one year, until August 1933.

It wasn't just hard for county residents to pay taxes. It must have been difficult for the tax collectors to collect the taxes. In August, the commissioners notified nine elected tax collectors in the county that they still owed the county some money.

During those years, the school system was on a county-by-county basis. This meant that the board of commissioners would have a say in how education money was spent. Part of their role was to purchase clothing and shoes for students.

According to the commissioners' meeting notes, that process became a little stricter. The school board had to requisition the items from the county and could not proceed to buy anything until it was approved by at least two commissioners.

The commissioners also noted an unusual phenomenon: items were missing from the courthouse. It would seem typewriters, blankets and janitorial supplies had been taken after the courthouse was closed. The commissioners figured that part of the problem was due to the policy of leaving the courthouse unlocked so people could use the restrooms. Access to the restrooms was curtailed after 6:00 p.m.

The death of Jefferson County treasurer Grant Sheafnocker in September 1932 led to the appointment of Richard E. Reitz by Governor Gifford Pinchot. It was an appointment that was short in duration but long on antagonism.

According to a family history written by Mary Ruth Reitz, when her uncle took office he found the "records full of unsubstantiated expenditures." Numerous county employees had been given advances on their pay, and major payments and advances had been made in Sheafnocker's name even after his death! Reitz refused to pay the county's bills until he had been given detailed information about the expenditures.

The commissioners did not comply, and Reitz did not pay the bills until ordered to do so by the Court of Common Pleas. The situation came to the attention of Brookville newspaper editor W.N. Conrad, who attempted to get information on the county's expenditures. According to the Reitz history, Conrad was barred from obtaining the information and was "shoved" by one of the commissioners.

Reitz argued that as the county's treasurer he was covered by a fidelity bond if he was required to handle state and county funds, especially sinking funds. The sinking fund was established to pay the bonds sold in 1927 for the renovation of the courthouse. The annual tax levy put money into the fund, which drew interest.

The state had adopted a law that allowed the counties to set up a sinking fund commission. In Jefferson County, that commission was composed of the three commissioners and three others they appointed. They could, if approved by the majority of the board, use the sinking fund money for other purposes. And they did.

In November, the commissioners raided the sinking fund and moved $10,000 into the county's checking account. Reitz, apparently sensing that he was being asked to do something not quite legal, vanished. The commissioners "sought him in his office several times" and made "inquiries upon the street," but the treasurer was no where to be found.

In December 1932, the commissioners had an open discussion on the condition of the county's finances. Since the county's treasury was "nearly exhausted," and to save "unnecessary interest," the commissioners recalled a part of the loan they had made to the poor fund. The county now had $10,000 to enter the new year. That did not carry the county through the first quarter.

In March 1933, Reid told the commissioners that the county's funds were "almost exhausted." Contributing to this cash flow problem was Reitz, who refused to turn over any tax money raised for the sinking fund or the poor tax to the commissioners. In effect, Reitz turned off the money tap.

The dispute between Reitz and the commissioners continued through several court appeals until Reitz was jailed by Judge William T. Darr for contempt. Reitz was sentenced to serve five days, but the Pennsylvania Supreme Court ordered his release after serving three days of his sentence.

In November, the county was once more faced with an empty treasury. This time, a larger loan was arranged from the Citizens National Bank for $8,000.

Reitz ran for a full term as treasurer in the 1934 election but lost. Reitz refused to turn over the keys to his office when he learned that the new treasurer had not taken his oath on time or obtained the required bond. He was forcibly removed from the office. (Reitz later ran for county sheriff on the unique slogan "Send Dick Reitz back to jail." He lost.)

The county's finances did not improve in 1935, and for the third straight year, the salaries of the county's employees were frozen. The county was able to repay all of its short-term loans and entered 1935 with no "floating indebtedness." That rosy situation did not last long.

A $10,000 loan from the Punxsutawney National Back on January 7 put the county back on the same treadmill. An additional $10,000 loan was arranged through the Citizens National Bank in Big Run for the Poor District.

The short-term borrowing continued, and by April, the county had amassed $35,000 in floating debt. This did not sit well with county voters. In the following election, McQuown decided not to run again, and Reid lost his seat. A new board—Sutter, G.C. Shuckers and S. Emory Kuntz—was elected, as was a new treasurer, Harvey Bowers.

The county continued to struggle with finances for another six years. The pattern of short-term borrowing and reducing salaries and services was repeated again and again until the financial situation took a back seat to a far greater drama, World War II.

## Renovation and Tragedy

Jefferson County commissioners Sam Hunter, John Daugherty and Perry Wingart watched in dismay as the steady rain collected in pools in the basement of the county courthouse continued to rise. Like Noah and his ark, they realized that the time had come to do something about conditions in the aging courthouse.

The rising water endangered the county's records, which were stored in the lower level of the courthouse. Worse, at least to the county employees, was the condition of the furnace. The water rose high enough to snuff out the fires beneath the steam boilers, ruining the system.

In 1922, the commissioners had authorized an Oil City, Pennsylvania architect to examine the cost of renovating and enlarging the courthouse. Despite the urging of three grand juries and a court order by Judge William Darr, no action had been taken until the winter of 1926. Every board of commissioners understood that fixing the courthouse would be popular but paying for it would be political suicide.

The winter of '26 was an unusually wet one, and the damage caused by the encroaching water underscored the need for action. As a stopgap, small stoves were installed in almost every room, causing unpleasant (if not toxic) fumes. The stoves were not vented and presented a clear fire hazard.

A letter to the editor of the *Brookville Republican* detailed the deplorable conditions at the courthouse. The "citizen" said that the present courthouse "is inadequate…The heating system is abominable. In the morning the courtroom is chilly and in the afternoon, too hot; an incubator for colds and a general health menace."

"Citizen" found other reasons for concern. "The toilets are barbarous and the drinking water for the court served from an old wooden keg into a scummy glass pitcher and a microby glass that has served for more than a decade."

The commissioners found themselves between the proverbial rock and hard place. They pulled the four-year-old plans off the shelf and paid

An office in the Jefferson County Courthouse prior to the 1927 remodeling.

Emmett E. Bailey $8,000 to update the plans for the work. What Bailey proposed was a complete overhaul of the original 1868 structure and the addition of a new wing that would run parallel to Main Street and at right angles to the existing building. The courtroom itself would be shortened and a third floor added, without raising the height of the old building.

The old jail, long a sore spot with county residents, would be razed, and the eight cells would be built into the basement of the new wing, right below the sheriff's office.

When the commissioners announced the renovation plan, it sparked a storm of controversy. Many people felt that the building project was much too large for a county with a shrinking tax and population base. The project carried a price tag of $300,000 that was to be financed through a series of short-term bonds.

The *Brookville American* said that the decision was "planning to care for the county's official domicile for the next 50 years." The alternative, said the newspaper, was for an expenditure of $50,000 for a "makeshift."

The opinion of the people was split, and this was evidenced in the vote by the board of commissioners. Daugherty and Hunter voted for the project, but Wingert was opposed. Each side had their proponents, and each waged a battle to make their views official.

Almost immediately, the forces against the project filed a petition signed by three thousand people, which urged the county to stop the work. In March 1927, Judge Darr, who had once ordered the county to renovate the building, heard the appeal and upheld the project.

The opponents filed an injunction and hired some of the best lawyers in the county, including famed trial attorney Charles Margiotti. Judge Parker in Venango County heard the case at the request of Judge Darr.

In his ruling, Judge Parker found the opposition arguments incredible. On one hand, Parker said, the argument called for stopping the project on the grounds that the county could not afford the debt. At the same time, it was proposed to tear down the old building and erect a new one to replace it. Parker threw out the injunction.

Over one hundred interested residents attended the bid opening. The general contractor was Ray Richards of Brookville with a bid of $246, 590.67. The total cost of the project was estimated at $270,508.57.

The plans called for the erection of a thirty-six- by sixty-four-foot wing; the removal of the granite steps in the front of the courthouse, to be replaced with a semicircular staircase; an entrance on the ground floor beneath the steps; the closing of the Pickering Street exit; the sheriff's office to be located at the southwest corner of the building; and a full basement.

The floor plan included space for the Farm Bureau, county detective, jury commissioner, large vaults, multiple restrooms and the county school superintendent's office. The courtroom was to be shortened by twelve feet and modern seats would be added along with a judge's chambers, a small courtroom, the district attorney's office, a balcony at the far end of the courtroom and a provision for women jurors who were "currently enduring makeshift quarters."

In March 1927, an official groundbreaking ceremony was held. It was estimated that the work would be completed in about one year.

Richards wasted little time getting to work. Excavation for the new wing started in March and ran into problems. The rains came and the large hole in the ground filled rapidly. The hole was right under the office window of Jefferson County treasurer Harry Truman and inevitably was dubbed "Truman's swimming pool." The earth taken from the courthouse excavation was hauled down to the old fairgrounds, where it would become the base for the Little League fields along the Sandy Lick Creek.

Richards survived the rain (and the jibes) and moved forward rapidly. The pace of the work did not prevent him from observing that the original builders "knew something about how to build."

The interior of the building was also to be extensively remodeled. When it began, it soon became apparent that the workmen and the workers could not occupy the same space. The county employees had to go. The *Brookville Republican* editor said that the old courthouse "looked like Japan after the earthquake."

The commissioners required a large space and found it in the Park Auditorium building. The county would pay $7,000 for a one-year lease. Some of that money was used to install a pine floor, windows and a furnace.

During April 1927, county employees were engaged in packaging records and moving furniture to the temporary county headquarters. The move was accompanied by a tragedy.

The row offices of Jefferson County in the White Elephant, 1927.

Levi Plyer, a seventy-three-year-old janitor, was helping to erect the tall shelves in what was to be the Law Library at the Park Auditorium. He and a co-worker were balanced on chairs when Plyler slipped, falling onto the other chair and breaking his neck. He left behind a wife and ten children.

In spite of the tragedy, the work continued, and by May the court furniture was moved onto the auditorium's stage. Many of the county's records were moved to the First Methodist Church, which stands just behind the courthouse.

The work on the new wing became more dramatic when the cement was poured in early April and the steel bars for the jail put in place. "Neat slices" were opened in the rear of the old building to allow steel beams to be inserted into the old building, providing added strength. A new roof was made of "fireproof" materials.

Richards also had the contract for the removal of the old jail. The jail had been condemned, and the examiners would not guarantee it against imminent collapse. That may have been a factor in the decision of an inmate to escape. On May 19, 1927, he squeezed through a crack in the brick and escaped. (He was captured in a farmer's barn the next day.) Soon afterward, the remaining prisoners were removed to the Clarion County Jail until the work was completed.

The demolition of the jail was one of the easier components of the project. Richards's workmen could push over large sections of the wall using only a board. One item that required a little more excitement was the discovery of an old safe found in the jail. It had once belonged to the late Squire John J. Walker. No one had the combination so a safecracker was called in. In the presence of Judge Darr, Congressman N.L. Strong and a host of curious onlookers, the safe was opened. If the county commissioners were hoping for a hidden treasure, they were disappointed. All that the safe contained was twenty-five pennies, some cancelled checks and few records.

The exterior of the addition was completed in the spring of 1928. Soon the Reitz Furniture Company delivered $62,554 worth of new furnishings. The installation of the mahogany furniture in the courtroom balcony required the skilled supervision of the manufacturer's representative.

Visitors to the courthouse were impressed with what they saw. The third floor was painted red, the second floor brown and the third level green. The walls were covered with "muslin with a mottled finish." The second floor, above the marble, was painted in a robin's egg blue.

The courtroom was truly inspiring. Although the ceiling had been lowered and the courtroom shortened, the addition of the judge's chambers and the small courtroom made up for the change. The pilasters added a sense of height to the room, and the material used between the pilasters, "zenetherm," resembled marble.

The exterior was not neglected. Architect C.S. Ferguson met with several ladies groups to design the landscaping. The ground from the new wing sloped eight feet to Main Street with a walk stretching from the sheriff's office on the southwest corner to the street. A barberry hedge was planted along the new retaining wall, and it was suggested that a Scotch pine tree be planted to serve as a community Christmas tree. Space was left in the center of the courtyard for a planned war memorial.

At the commencement of the project, the editor of the *Republican* stated, "Doubtless the commissioners will come in for some criticism for proceeding with the reconstruction of the courthouse. It is a big undertaking and one on which snap judgment should not be taken. The reconstruction should make the courthouse serviceable for the next half century."

The editor was correct on both counts. The commissioners were held up to criticism. Both Hunter and Daugherty lost their reelection bids. The county received more than a half century of service from the 1927 remodeling. No major project was attempted until 2008, when a new board of commissioners authorized a complete upgrade, again on a split vote. Only this time the price tag was a bit larger: $5 million. Hopefully, this effort will also stand the test of time.

# Bibliography


*Brookville American.* Editions 1916 through 1990.

*Brookville Republican.* Editions 1856 through 1940.

Cunningham Memorial Library, Terre Haute, Indiana.

*Jeffersonian Democrat.* Editions 1835 through 1990.

McKnight, William J. *History of Jefferson County, Pennsylvania: Her Pioneers and People, 1800–1915.* 2 vols. Chicago, IL: J.H. Beers & Company, 1917.

Scott, Kate M. *History of Jefferson County, Pennsylvania.* Syracuse, NY: D. Mason & Co., 1888.

# About the Author

Randon Bartley is a past president of the Jefferson County Historical Society and a current member of the board of directors of Historic Brookville, Inc. He served as the chairman for the Jefferson County Sesquicentennial and was named as a Penn Ambassador by the Pennsylvania House of Representatives. He is a historical interpreter for the National Park Service at the Gettysburg, Antietam and Richmond National Battlefield Parks. Bartley has had articles published in a number of national periodicals. He has been the editor of the *Jeffersonian Democrat* in Brookville for over twenty years.